053205

NEW DIRECTIONS FOR COMMUNITY COLLEGES

Arthur M. Cohen Florence B. Brawer
EDITOR-IN-CHIEF ASSOCIATE EDITOR

R. Dean Gerdeman
PUBLICATION COORDINATOR

Community College Faculty: Characteristics, Practices, and Challenges

Charles L. Outcalt
University of California–Los Angeles

EDITOR

D1114584

Number 118, Summer 2002

JOSSEY-BASS
San Francisco

ERIC®

Clearinghouse for Community Colleges

COMMUNITY COLLEGE FACULTY: CHARACTERISTICS, PRACTICES, AND CHALLENGES
Charles L. Outcalt (ed.)
New Directions for Community Colleges, no. 118
Arthur M. Cohen, Editor-in-Chief
Florence B. Brawer, Associate Editor

New Directions for Community Colleges is indexed in Current Index to Journals in Education (ERIC).

Microfilm copies of issues and articles are available in 16mm and 35mm, as well as microfiche in 105mm, through University Microfilms Inc., 300 North Zeeb Road, Ann Arbor, Michigan 48106-1346.

ISSN 0194-3081   electronic ISSN 1534-2891   ISBN 0-7879-6328-3

NEW DIRECTIONS FOR COMMUNITY COLLEGES is part of The Jossey-Bass Higher and Adult Education Series and is published quarterly by Wiley Subscription Services, Inc., A Wiley Company, at Jossey-Bass, 989 Market Street, San Francisco, California 94103-1741, in association with the ERIC Clearinghouse for Community Colleges. Periodicals postage paid at San Francisco, California, and at additional mailing offices. POSTMASTER: Send address changes to New Directions for Community Colleges, Jossey-Bass, 989 Market Street, San Francisco, California 94103-1741.

SUBSCRIPTIONS cost $66.00 for individuals and $142.00 for institutions, agencies, and libraries. Prices subject to change.

THE MATERIAL in this publication is based on work sponsored wholly or in part by the Office of Educational Research and Improvement, U.S. Department of Education, under contract number ED-99-CO-0010. Its contents do not necessarily reflect the views of the Department or any other agency of the U.S. Government.

EDITORIAL CORRESPONDENCE should be sent to the Editor-in-Chief, Arthur M. Cohen, at the ERIC Clearinghouse for Community Colleges, University of California, 3051 Moore Hall, Box 951521, Los Angeles, California 90095-1521. All manuscripts receive anonymous reviews by external referees.

Cover photograph © Rene Sheret, After Image, Los Angeles, California, 1990.

Printed in the United States of America on acid-free recycled paper containing at least 20 percent postconsumer waste.

CONTENTS

EDITOR'S NOTES

The importance of community college faculty for higher education cannot be overestimated: Huber (1998) reports that community college faculty constitute 31 percent of all U.S. higher education faculty, teaching 39 percent of all higher education students and 46 percent of all first-year students. Accordingly, the way in which the two-year college faculty teach and interact with their students has a profound effect on the overall conduct of American higher education.

As the principal point of contact between students and institutions, community college faculty are central to all issues of college role and function. Since the maturation of the community college system in the 1960s, researchers have investigated the means by which community college faculty deliver their most important service—teaching—to their students. Several of these researchers, including Garrison (1967) and Cohen and Brawer (1972, 1977, 1984) have undertaken broad analyses of the relationship between the community college professoriate's development as a distinct profession and its professional practice. These studies demonstrate a link between the characteristics of the community college professoriate and its service to its student clientele. Accordingly, faculty activities, their environments and professional relationships, as well as their attitudes and values, deserve continual examination.

As useful as the studies noted above can be for those who seek to understand the community college professoriate, they require updating. In the past twenty-five years the community colleges have changed in many dimensions. They have broadened the types of students they serve, established new statements of mission, and extended their activities into a wider array of community services. Many have begun characterizing themselves as community development centers. Furthermore, many of their leaders have adopted the idea that the colleges are participants in the global economy through attracting international students and building courses to be beamed to students in other countries. Distance education has become a growing element within community colleges, which are more likely than other higher education sectors to employ distance technology in planning and broadcasting curriculum.

At the same time, the community college student body and faculty have changed. Enrollments grew from 3.8 million in 1975 to 5.3 million

The Center for the Study of Community Colleges faculty survey described herein was made possible through the generous support of the Spencer Foundation Small Grants Program and the University of California-Berkeley's Center for the Study of Higher Education.

twenty years later, even while the number of colleges changed hardly at all. Student demographics shifted, with the number identifying themselves as white falling from 80 percent to 70 percent. The faculty increased from 160,000 to 270,000. Part-timers now account for nearly 65 percent of all community college faculty. In sum, larger colleges with an increasing proportion of students of color meet a faculty composed in large part of part-time instructors.

Several of the chapters in this volume draw on a survey of community college faculty administered by the Center for the Study of Community Colleges (CSCC) in 2000. In the interest of economy, it would be useful to outline, briefly, the means by which the survey was administered. In addition, it would be helpful to offer, in brief terms, the sample's demographic characteristics.

With the CSCC survey, a national, random sample of community college faculty responded to questions concerning their backgrounds, practices, and attitudes. It is important to note that the survey updated a similar study of humanities instructors conducted by the CSCC in 1975, and so some longitudinal comparisons for humanities faculty can be made between 1975 and 2000.

In May 2000, CSCC staff invited 240 college presidents, chosen at random, to participate in the study. If college presidents declined to participate, another college of similar size (as measured by student FTE) was invited in its place. By September 2000, 478 colleges had been invited to participate; of these, 70 declined to take part, 156 agreed to participate, and the remainder did not respond. No inferences can be drawn from the ways in which institutions responded to the invitation.

Community college presidents were asked to appoint a local facilitator to serve as the designated on-campus contact person and to take responsibility for administering the survey on the campus. Facilitators sent CSCC staff a Fall 2000 course schedule, which was used to select the faculty sample. By late September, course schedules had been received from 114 of the 156 participating colleges. To generate a sample of approximately 1,500 completed surveys, 2,292 respondents were chosen at random by selecting every nth class listed from the course schedules (the value of n varied by the size of the community college).

In early October 2000, survey packets were mailed to local facilitators, who distributed them on their campuses and retrieved them from respondents via an anonymous double-envelope mailing system. By January 2001, 1,531 of the 2,292 surveys sent in October had been returned. Five colleges, with ninety-five surveys among them, chose to withdraw from the study between the time of their presidents' decisions to participate and the survey deadline. An additional 204 surveys were deemed undeliverable by the local facilitators, almost always because courses were changed between the time the schedules were printed in the spring and the beginning of the Fall semester. In total, then, 1,531 of 1,993 valid surveys were returned, for a response rate of 76.8 percent.

The survey instrument consists of a questionnaire of approximately two hundred questions in eight pages, with 75 percent of survey questions being exact or near-exact repetitions of questions asked on the 1975 survey. Most survey questions are designed to illuminate one or more of several analytical categories concerning major categories of faculty practices and attitudes, including demographics, curriculum and instruction, satisfaction, professional involvement, and concern for students. Many of the chapters in this volume explore one or more dimensions of the practices and attitudes with which these constructs are concerned, while others draw on additional data to illuminate other aspects of the professoriate.

Before proceeding to this volume's chapters, it would be useful to provide a brief examination of the demographic characteristics of the CSCC sample. In the CSCC study, men and women are found to comprise the faculty in nearly equal measure. This result is slightly different from figures reported by the National Center for Education statistics, which reports that just over half (54.7 percent) of community college faculty are men (U.S. Department of Education, 1997, Table 227). White instructors, at 86.6 percent, form a majority of respondents; African-Americans, at 4.8 percent, being the next largest racial/ethnic group. These findings are consistent with those of Palmer and Zimbler (2000), whose analysis of 1992 data show that 86.1 percent of the community college professoriate is white/Caucasian.

Respondent ages fall into a nearly normal distribution around the range of forty-five to fifty-four years old. Over one-third (38.2 percent) of instructors are between forty-five and fifty-four years of age, with the vast majority (83.4 percent) between thirty-five and sixty-four. The bulk of respondents have not served in an administrative role for any length of time. Most (68.3 percent) respondents report that they have never taught in a four-year college or university. A sizable minority of respondents (37.9 percent) report having taught in a secondary school. However, as noted below, this figure is substantially lower than in the past, demonstrating the decreasing significance of high schools as sources for community college instructors.

Full-timers form 69.5 percent of the total sample for the current study. This figure constitutes a clear overrepresentation of full-timers. (For example, Palmer and Zimbler, 2000, find that full-timers formed only 38 percent of the community college professoriate in 1992.) The proportion of full-timers is attributable to the sampling procedure followed in this study, as outlined above. Most respondents neither have nor seek doctorates. Only 15.6 percent report holding a doctorate, and an even smaller percentage (8.8 percent) are pursuing this type of degree. The sample is not quite evenly divided between liberal arts and occupational instructors, with members of the former group holding a majority.

Not only do Cohen and Brawer note a tendency toward greater demographic diversity in their 1977 analysis, but other scholars since (Palmer and Zimbler, 2000) have observed this trend. The CSCC survey, in keeping with these findings, shows that community college faculty are more diverse in 2000 than in 1975, and are closer to being representative of the U.S. population in general. Women in particular have made gains since the 1975 survey, and, at least according to the results of the current survey, have achieved parity with men. The proportion of faculty of color has increased as well, with the percentage of humanities respondents identifying themselves as white/Caucasian falling from 90.6 percent in 1975 to 79.7 percent in 2000.

The faculty are in general older than they were in 1975, most probably because of hiring patterns within the community college system. In addition, they are more experienced, with longer periods of service to their profession. In 1975, 58.2 percent of humanities faculty had served for over five years; by 2000, this figure has climbed to 74.0 percent. This trend persists for all instructors, with 72.2 percent of them having served for longer than five years. This lengthening is almost certainly related to the pattern by which the community college system was developed, with rapid growth in the 1960s followed by a period of relative stability. Relatively few community college instructors have served as administrators, but those who have demonstrate the same trend toward a longer period of service in 2000 than in 1975.

While nearly 60 percent of community college instructors in the humanities taught in the secondary schools in 1975, only 45.4 percent did so by 2000, with an even smaller percentage of community college instructors in general (37.9 percent) teaching in the high schools. Among humanities instructors, 19.9 percent in the 2000 study have taught at the four-year level for five or more years, while only 14.5 percent of those in the 1975 study did so. In short, the high schools are much less important sources of community college faculty than they were in 1975, and the colleges and universities are more important.

As noted above, the chapters in this volume explore the characteristics, practices, and attitudes of the community college professoriate from a diverse array of perspectives. Each chapter yields insights and analyses into discrete aspects of the professoriate; taken together, these chapters offer a nuanced, finely grained portrait of community college faculty.

In Chapter One, Palmer analyzes disciplinary differences in instructional practice, using the NSOPF:99 dataset. With Chapter Two, Lee explores community college faculty's uses of professional reference groups. Brookfield, in Chapter Three, discusses the use of critical reflection to improve instructional practice among community college faculty. Schuetz, in Chapter Four, Kozeracki, in Chapter Five, and Leslie and Gappa, in Chapter Six, explore the significance of differences in employment status. However, the focus of these chapters differs: Schuetz focuses specifically on differences in instructional practice on the basis of employment status, while Kozeracki examines faculty attitudes toward students, and Leslie and Gappa look more broadly at overall similarities and differences between full-time and part-time faculty. Chapters Seven and Eight analyze the experience of minority faculty: Hagedorn and

Laden investigate working conditions and attitudes for women faculty, with a particular focus on women of color, while Bower combines qualitative and quantitative data to examine the experience of ethnic/racial minority faculty. In Chapter Nine, Murray discusses the effectiveness (and lack thereof) of faculty professional development programs. In Chapters Ten and Eleven, Weisman, Marr, and Outcalt look to the future for community college faculty: Weisman and Marr explore issues of community within community colleges, and Outcalt offers recommendations for research and practice drawn from the CSCC survey. Finally, Fleming's Sources and Information chapter provides details on additional resources for further study of the community college professoriate.

Charles L. Outcalt

Editor

References

Cohen, A. M., and Brawer, F. B. *Confronting Identity: The Community College Instructor.* Englewood Cliffs, N.J.: Prentice-Hall, 1972.

Cohen, A. M., and Brawer, F. B. *The Two-Year College Instructor Today.* New York: Holt, Rinehart and Winston, 1977.

Cohen, A. M., and Brawer, F. B. *The Collegiate Function of Community Colleges: Fostering Higher Learning through Curriculum and Student Transfer.* San Francisco: Jossey-Bass, 1984.

Garrison, R. H. *Junior College Faculty: Issues and Problems; A Preliminary National Appraisal.* Washington, D.C.: American Association of Community and Junior Colleges, 1967.

Huber, M. T. *Community College Faculty Attitudes and Trends, 1997* (R309A60001; NCPI-4–03). National Center for Postsecondary Improvement, Stanford, California, 1998.

Palmer, J. C., and Zimbler, L. J. *Instructional Faculty and Staff in Public 2-year Colleges.* Washington, D.C.: U.S. Department of Education, Office of Educational Research and Improvement, 2000.

U.S. Department of Education. *Digest of Education Statistics* (NCES 98–015). Washington, D.C.: U.S. Department of Education, 1997.

CHARLES L. OUTCALT *earned his Ph.D. from the Graduate School of Education and Information Studies at the University of California–Los Angeles in 2002. His dissertation offers a profile of community college faculty.*

PART ONE

Profiles of Community College Faculty

1

Community college teachers are members of different disciplinary groups; they are mathematicians, biologists, nurses, and accountants. Data from the 1999 National Survey of Postsecondary Faculty offer an updated look at how faculty members in different disciplines approach their work.

Disciplinary Variations in the Work of Full-Time Faculty Members

James C. Palmer

Lost amid perennial discussions of the community college's social and economic roles is the fundamental fact that the institution's main purpose is to help students learn academic disciplines and career skills. The colleges are structured accordingly, divided by subject area into departments or units. Those who do the institution's core work—teaching—are hired within those departments as subject specialists who connect students to specific bodies of knowledge.

Given this disciplinary structure and purpose, it is reasonable to expect that faculty work will vary across academic fields. Scholars have long noted that faculty lives are defined largely by the competing demands of the institution on the one hand and their disciplines on the other (Clark, 1997). Even within the community college, which has a teaching emphasis and hence exerts a stronger institutional pull on faculty members than research-focused universities, disciplinary affiliations have a noticeable influence (Cohen and Brawer, 1977; Outcalt, 2001; Palmer, 1992, 2000).

The U.S. Department of Education's 1999 National Survey of Postsecondary Faculty (NSOPF-99) offers the latest national picture of the American professoriate, allowing an updated look into disciplinary variations in the work of community college teachers. The survey database provides information on how faculty members conducted their work in the fall of 1998. This chapter draws on the database to profile full-time community college faculty respondents in eleven disciplinary groups: business (10 percent), education (3 percent), engineering and computer sciences (9 percent), fine arts (6 percent), health sciences (12 percent), human services (4 percent), humanities (17 percent), life sciences (6 percent), in natural, physical sciences, and math (12 percent), in social sciences (10 percent), and in vocational education (11 percent). Percentages refer to the proportion of the sample composed of faculty members in each discipline; weights used in the database yield an approximate total of 89,000 full-time community college faculty members who indicate that teaching credit courses is their primary responsibility. For a complete description of categories, see NSOPF-99 Codebook, available at [http://nces.ed.gov/das/htm/das/pf9.html]. Results of the survey show an overall tendency toward instructional conservatism; regardless of discipline, faculty members taught largely on a face-to-face basis with students and relied heavily on lectures. But within this overarching framework lay significant disciplinary variations along four lines: (1) academic and employment histories; (2) approaches to instruction, (3) methods used to assess student work, and (4) scholarship outside of teaching. (All differences reported here emerged in multiple-comparison t-tests (p <.05); the Bonferroni adjustment to significance levels was used because of the large, weighted sample size.)

Academic and Employment Histories

Data on the highest degree earned by the respondents, on their employment in higher education, and on their concurrent employment elsewhere (Table 1.1) suggest a key point of disciplinary difference: the tendency of faculty in some disciplines to be more connected to the academic world than faculty in other disciplines. This is evident in the respondents' academic histories; most (61 percent) hold master's degrees, but some have proceeded further through formal education than others. For example, faculty members in the humanities, life sciences, in the natural sciences, physical sciences, and mathematics, and in the social sciences are more likely to hold doctorates or first professional degrees than their colleagues in career areas (business, education, engineering and computer sciences, health sciences, human services, and vocational fields). Conversely, teachers in engineering and computer sciences, fine arts, health sciences, and vocational fields are more likely than those in the remaining areas to have proceeded no further than the baccalaureate.

In addition, faculty members vary in terms of their exposure to the world of work outside of academe. Not surprisingly, those teaching in vocational programs are less likely than those in the humanities to work outside of higher education (32 percent vs. 52 percent). Health sciences instructors are even less likely to work solely within colleges or universities; only 20 percent have spent their entire work lives in higher education, significantly less of a percentage than teachers in all other categories except vocational education, education, human services, and engineering and computer sciences. The vocational and health sciences categories clearly represent disciplinary groupings in which "real world" settings play a relatively large role in the preparation of community college teachers. Faculty members in both

Table 1.1. Selected Indicators of Educational Background, Employment in Higher Education, and Current Outside Employment for Full-Time Community College Faculty Members, Fall 1998

	Highest Degree Earned			Employment in Higher Education		Current Outside Employment	
All Full-Time Faculty Members	Percent Indicating 1st Professional or Doctorate 20 percent	Percent Indicating Master's Degree 61 percent	Percent Indicating Bachelor's Degree or Less 19 percent	Percent Who Have Worked Only in Higher Education 39 percent	Percent Whose Previous Employment had been Outside of Higher Education 37 percent	Percent Engaged in Consulting 24 percent	Percent with Other, Nonconsulting Job 34 percent
Business	10	75	15	40	35	31	31
Education	13	76	11	29	38	21	39
Engineering and computer sciences	11	51	39	33	42	43	29
Fine arts	14	69	17	44	31	32	47
Health sciences	6	63	31	20	52	21	46
Human services	11	83	6	41	36	15	31
Humanities	31	68	1	52	23	17	29
Life sciences	39	53	8	46	25	13	31
Natural, physical sciences, and math	31	66	4	41	30	7	30
Social sciences	38	58	5	41	31	28	39
Vocational education	10	28	62	32	59	36	29

Source: NSOPF-99, U.S. Department of Education Data Analysis System (http://nces.ed.gov/das/index.html). Data reported here and in the other tables in this chapter summarize responses from full-time faculty members who indicated that teaching credit courses was their primary responsibility. The weighted sample size for respondents who meet these criteria is approximately 89,000.

categories are more likely than those in the humanities, life sciences, in natural sciences, physical sciences, and mathematics, and in social sciences to have been previously employed outside of the academy.

Finally, the varying importance of the world beyond the campus can also be seen in data on concurrent employment outside of the college. Again, the health sciences category stands out. In contrast to those teaching the humanities, a larger percentage of the health sciences faculty (46 percent vs. 29 percent) report at least some outside employment that does not involve consulting. The engineering and computer sciences group has the largest proportion of teachers (43 percent) who earn outside money through consulting, a proportion significantly higher than for those in health sciences, human services, the humanities, life sciences, and in natural sciences, physical sciences, and mathematics.

Approaches to Instruction

Despite varying levels of connection to the academic world, faculty members across disciplines hold to traditional instructional approaches (Table 1.2). When asked about their use of "lecture/discussion," 88 percent overall indicate that it is the primary instructional method in some or all of their classes. The data offer some evidence that faculty in career-related areas rely less frequently on lecture, due probably to the hands-on work that career courses sometimes entail. Faculty members in vocational programs are less likely to use the lecture/discussion method as a primary class medium than are their colleagues in the liberal arts. Teachers in other career-related areas (business, education, engineering and computer sciences, health sciences, and human services) also exhibit slightly lower figures than these four academic subject clusters, although the differences are not statistically significant.

Faculty use of instructional methods other than lecture/discussion drop off precipitously. No disciplinary variations emerge in the use of fieldwork. However, significant differences between the disciplinary clusters do emerge when faculty are asked about the use of "labs, clinics, or problems sessions." Here the career-academic split is again evident, at least partially, with instructors in the humanities, social sciences, and in natural sciences, physical sciences, and mathematics reporting significantly lower use of these methods than the instructors in engineering and computer sciences, health sciences, vocational programs, and the fine arts.

Significant differences are also apparent in the faculty's use of distance-learning technologies. Predictably, teachers in the engineering and computer sciences category lead the way, with those teaching business courses following closely behind. One-third of the faculty members in the engineering and computer sciences group report that one or more of their courses are taught via some form of distance education, a figure significantly higher than for all other categories except business and education. Almost

Table 1.2. Percentage of Full-Time Community College Faculty Members Using Selected Instructional Modes as the Primary Instructional Method in Some or All of Their Classes, Fall 1998, by Primary Teaching Field

Instructional Methods

All Full-Time Faculty Members	*Some Form of Distance* Education (Including Computer, TV, or Other Methods) 17 percent*	*Computer 11 percent*	*Lab, Clinic, or Problem Session 38 percent*	*Field Work 7 percent*	*Seminar 9 percent*	*Lecture/Discussion 88 percent*
Business	29	21	37	7	6	90
Education	18	13	30	15	20	87
Engineering and computer sciences	34	33	55	6	10	83
Fine arts	8	4	55	17	4	81
Health sciences	13	6	53	12	11	88
Human services	17	10	40	8	7	87
Humanities	14	9	19	4	12	93
Life sciences	10	5	47	6	4	97
Natural, physical sciences, and math	13	5	20	3	12	95
Social sciences	16	6	19	5	10	93
Vocational education	12	8	61	4	7	72

Source: NSOPF-99, U.S. Department of Education Data Analysis System (http://nces.ed.gov/das/index.html)

*Referred to as "non-face-to-face instruction".

one-third (29 percent) of the teachers in the business category teach at least one course using distance-learning technologies, outstripping the percentages reported for fine arts, life sciences, vocational programs, and for natural sciences, physical sciences, and mathematics. One-fifth (21 percent) of the business faculty members indicate that one or more courses are taught via computer, significantly more than the number of those teaching in the fine arts, health sciences, life sciences, social sciences, and in natural sciences, physical sciences, and mathematics.

Assessing Student Work

In addition to insights on the mode of instruction, the NSOPF-99 survey sheds light on faculty use of various assessment techniques (Table 1.3). Respondents were asked, for example, about their use of competency-based grading on the one hand and grading curves on the other. Results suggest that faculty members in some areas are more likely than those in other categories to use criterion-based grading schemes rather than norm-referenced schemes. Faculty in the business, engineering, and health sciences fields are more likely than colleagues in humanities, life sciences, natural sciences, physical sciences, mathematics, and social sciences to indicate the use of competency-based grading in some or all courses. This again suggests a divide between career-related and academic fields. But the data regarding grading curves offer a less clear-cut picture. Teachers in the health sciences are less likely than teachers in all other categories to grade on a curve in all or some courses, although statistically significant differences are found only in relation to percentages for business, for natural sciences, physical sciences, and mathematics, and for social sciences. Nonetheless, the use of grading curves among health sciences faculty members in some or all courses is essentially the same as that reported by teachers in humanities (14 percent vs. 16 percent, respectively).

Disciplinary variations also emerge in the extent to which faculty members make student writing a part of the assessment process. Predictably, those in the natural sciences, physical sciences, and mathematics category are less likely than those in other groups to require term papers in some or all classes (although statistically significant differences emerge only in relation to the business, education, health sciences, humanities, life sciences, and social sciences categories). The natural sciences, physical sciences, and mathematics group is also less likely than teachers in most other categories to require multiple drafts of written work. Humanities faculty members, on the other hand, emphasize student writing relatively highly, exceeding all groups except human services in the use of essay mid-term or final examinations. Humanities faculty are also more likely than their colleagues in all other groups to require multiple drafts of written work. This is not surprising, given the fact that English teachers are included in the humanities group. In short, variations in faculty emphasis on writing as an assessment

Table 1.3. Percentage of Full-Time Community College Faculty Members Who Used Selected Assessment Techniques in Some or All of Their Classes, Fall 1998, by Primary Teaching Field

	Assessment Techniques							
All Full-Time Faculty Members	Competency-Based Grading 67 Percent	Grading on a Curve 25 Percent	Essay Mid-Terms or Final Exams 56 Percent	Multiple Drafts of Written Work 36 Percent	Short-Answer Mid-term or Final Exams 65 Percent	Multiple-Choice Mid-Term or Final Exams 73 Percent	Student Evaluations of Each Other's Work 47 Percent	Term/Research Papers 56 Percent
Business	66	31	57	42	69	84	48	58
Education	66	21	63	56	66	73	62	68
Engineering and computer sciences	77	27	55	27	74	71	52	54
Fine arts	72	29	63	24	65	61	57	51
Health sciences	77	14	35	35	49	95	54	61
Human services	66	25	60	26	76	84	58	59
Humanities	68	16	84	68	59	52	62	69
Life sciences	54	25	60	21	78	90	26	59
Natural, physical sciences, and math	51	37	41	15	66	53	23	35
Social sciences	51	30	62	32	62	82	41	65
Vocational education	84	23	39	31	71	82	41	40

Source: NSOPF-99, U.S. Department of Education Data Analysis System (http://nces.ed.gov/das/index.html)

criterion relate less to the career-academic dichotomy than to the very different material covered in mathematically oriented courses on the one hand and English courses on the other. (However, teachers in natural sciences and physical sciences and mathematics are no more likely to use multiple-choice exams than are teachers in the humanities. Faculty members in both groups make little use of these exams.)

Besides placing a relatively low emphasis on writing, teachers in mathematically and scientifically oriented courses also appear less likely to involve students in the assessment of one another's work. Faculty teaching natural sciences, physical sciences, and mathematics, along with colleagues in the life sciences, are less likely to allow these peer evaluations in some or all of their classes than teachers in all other categories except education and the social sciences. This suggests disciplinary variations in the student-teacher relationship, with faculty members in some disciplines taking a more directive stance toward students than colleagues in other fields.

Out-of-Class Scholarship

Although teaching is the faculty's primary responsibility, many community college faculty engage in other forms of scholarship (Table 1.4). Among the full-time community college teachers profiled in this chapter, 33 percent indicate that they are engaged in "professional research, proposal writing, creative writing, or creative works"; 30 percent have published at least once in the two years preceding the NSOPF-99 survey; and 41 percent have completed at least one presentation, exhibition, or performance. Just over half (51 percent) of the out-of-class research, writing, or creative work that the faculty members worked on during the fall of 1998 was related to textbook production or to the design of curricula and instructional programs.

These overall findings mask several variations, particularly between fine arts and the humanities on the one hand and career-related areas on the other. For example, the proportion of faculty members engaged in "professional research, proposal writing, creative writing, or creative works" is higher in the fine arts and the humanities than in business, engineering and in computer sciences, health sciences, and vocational programs. The split between academic and career fields also emerges in data on publications. The proportion of faculty who published at least one item in the two years prior to the survey is higher in the humanities than in business, engineering and computer sciences, health, human services, and vocational programs.

In addition, fine arts and humanities instructors are more likely to engage in "other" creative work (such as basic research or artistic creation) than their colleagues in business, engineering and computer sciences, health sciences, human services, vocational programs, and in natural sciences, physical sciences, and mathematics. However, the opposite trend applies in

Table 1.4. Indicators of Out-of-Class Scholarship Activities of Full-Time Community College Faculty Members, Fall 1998

	Percent Indicating Engagement in Professional Research, Proposal Writing, Creative Writing, or Creative Works 33 Percent	Primary Type of Research, Writing or Creative Work (includes only those currently engaged in such work)			Scholarly Products During the Past Two Years	
		Percent Indicating Work Related to Program/Curriculum Design or to Textbooks 51 Percent	Percent Indicating Applied, Policy, or Clinical Work 13 Percent	Percent Indicating Other Types of Creative Work 37 Percent	Percent Indicating at Least One Publication 30 Percent	Percent Indicating at Least One Presentation, Exhibition, or Performance 41 Percent
All Full-Time Faculty Members						
Business	20	73	13 percent	14 percent	26	37
Education	30	low n*	low n*	low n*	31	62
Engineering and computer sciences	23	83	5 percent	12 percent	22	37
Fine arts	53	25	2 percent	74 percent	27	46
Health sciences	25	63	15 percent	22 percent	23	40
Human services	35	low n*	low n*	low n*	22	38
Humanities	51	34	11 percent	54 percent	45	54
Life sciences	38	61	13 percent	26 percent	33	37
Natural, physical sciences, and math	31	59	23 percent	18 percent	35	39
Social sciences	35	37	15 percent	49 percent	34	39
Vocational education	25	63	21 percent	16 percent	22	28

Source: NSOPF-99, U.S. Department of Education Data Analysis System (http://nces.ed.gov/das/index.html)

*Numbers are too low for meaningful analysis

the case of out-of-class scholarship focusing on instructional programs, curricula, or textbooks. Thus it appears that instructors in career-related fields are more likely to focus their out-of-class scholarship on the production of instructional materials than on the other scholarly products.

Summary

Because the eleven categories employed in this analysis are broad, each encompassing several disciplines, the variations reported here do not adequately show how faculty work differs across subject areas. Further breakdown of these categories often yields insufficient numbers for comparison. In the few cases in which such breakdowns *are* possible, results are tantalizing. English and history, both within the humanities category, are examples. The vast majority of faculty members teaching English (83 percent) require students to write multiple drafts of written work, compared with only 23 percent of faculty teaching history. English and history teachers also differ in their use of multiple-choice examinations; 47 percent of the English faculty use such exams, compared with 72 percent of the history teachers.

Nonetheless, understanding differences across disciplines is useful, even across broad categories. First, it sheds light on the varying career paths that lead to full-time membership in community college faculties. Data on education and employment (Table 1.1) suggest that for some faculty members, notably those in the humanities and other academic fields, those paths tend to follow the traditional route of graduate school followed by employment as a teacher. For others (notably those in engineering and computer sciences, fine arts, health sciences, and vocational fields) teaching is likely to be an extension of work outside the academy. Those who teach in the two-year college represent a broad spectrum of the local community.

Second, appreciating disciplinary differences counters the tendency to discuss the community college enterprise as a homogeneous culture, thus guarding against the naïve application of faculty development programs that press the same instructional nostrums across disciplines. Community college faculty members are, after all, members of different disciplinary groups; they are mathematicians and biologists, nurses and accountants. Collective, faculty-driven efforts within these groups to improve teaching make sense and characterize such organizations as the American Mathematical Association of Two-Year Colleges, comprising those who teach lower-division mathematics [http://www.amatyc.org/], and the TWC21 group, which involves community college physics teachers in the study of pedagogy within their discipline (American Association of Physics Teachers, 2000).

Third, analyses of disciplinary variations within the faculty may lead to insights about potentially beneficial outliers—faculty members who buck prevailing trends in their own fields. For example, it is interesting to note that although most respondents in the natural sciences, physical sciences, and mathematics categories do not require students to write multiple drafts of written work, 15 percent *do* require multiple drafts in some or all of their classes

(Table 1.3). This represents a break from the norm that may enrich the student's educational experience. Additional research should be conducted to determine why faculty members divert from the norm and how institutions can support such innovation when it results in improved instruction.

Finally, understanding disciplinary variations may also lead to a more accurate picture of the differences in faculty work between the two-year and four-year colleges. Aggregate differences between these sectors are commonly reported in national analyses (Finkelstein, Seal, and Schuster, 1999). However, these aggregate sector comparisons mask variations by academic field. For example, analysis of the NSOPF-99 data shows that four-year college faculty who teach undergraduate students are more likely overall to require essay mid-term or final exams than are faculty members at two-year colleges (63 percent vs. 53 percent). But the reverse is true in engineering and computer sciences; in this area, faculty members from community colleges are more likely to use essay tests than colleagues in four-year colleges (55 percent vs. 49 percent). And in the case of health sciences, faculty use of essay examinations is essentially the same in both sectors.

Disciplinary variations should not be overstated. As the widespread use of the lecture/discussion method suggests, a large swath of tradition cuts across academic fields. Faculty are imbued in and contribute to that tradition, but they do so in their own ways within their own disciplinary subgroups. Understanding those subgroups is as important to understanding the community college as it is to understanding the flagship university.

References

American Association of Physics Teachers. *A Model for Reform. Two-Year Colleges in the 21st Century: Breaking Down Barriers.* Washington, D.C.: American Association of Physics Teachers, 2000.

Clark, B. R. "Small Worlds, Different Worlds. The Uniqueness and Troubles of American Academic Professions." *Daedalus,* 1997, *126*(4), 21–42.

Cohen, A. M., and Brawer, F. B. *The Two-Year College Instructor Today.* New York: Praeger, 1977.

Finkelstein, M. J., Seal, R., and Schuster, J. H. *New Entrants to the Full-Time Faculty of Higher Education Institutions* (NCES 98252). Washington, D.C.: National Center for Education Statistics, 1999.

Outcalt, C. "Faculty Attitudes Priorities and Values: Selected Findings From a National Survey of Community College Faculty members." Forum Presentation at the Convention of the American Association of Community Colleges, Chicago, April 5, 2001.

Palmer, J. C. "The Scholarly Activity of Community College Faculty: Findings of a National Survey." In J. C. Palmer and G. B. Vaughan (eds.), *Fostering a Climate for Faculty Scholarship at the Community College.* Washington, D.C.: American Association of Community and Junior Colleges, 1992.

Palmer, J. C. *Instructional Faculty and Staff in Public Two-Year Colleges* (NCES 2000–192). Washington, D.C.: National Center for Education Statistics, 2000.

JAMES C. PALMER *is professor of educational administration and foundations at Illinois State University.*

2

Understanding faculty reference groups is critical to understanding faculty values and behavior, as well as to introducing and implementing change efforts. This chapter focuses on the extent to which the university serves as a reference group for community college faculty and distinguishes notable differences by faculty characteristics and teaching fields.

University Reference Group Identification Among Community College Faculty

Jenny J. Lee

Faculty behaviors are a common measure of faculty workload, productivity, and responsibilities, observable indicators that, while helpful in understanding the performance of the institution, neglect to inform us of what drives these behaviors. A more imperative level of analysis concerns what influences faculty practice (as well as related values and beliefs). Examining faculty reference groups is key not only to understanding better the workings of the institution but also to tackling complex issues or initiating change. For community college faculty, discerning identification sources is difficult. Community college faculty comprise a heterogeneous mix of postsecondary teaching professionals with varying levels of degree attainment. Whether they make use of the secondary schools or the university as a role model is often ambiguous. Seidman (1985) suggests that the position of the community college faculty can be viewed as a "halfway step" between secondary-school and university faculties. While perhaps true decades ago, whether this view is common today remains to be evidenced. Therefore, a current understanding of community college faculty requires an investigation of the extent to which the university serves as a reference group for today's community college faculty.

James Palmer (see Chapter One) highlights notable differences in instructional practice among academic disciplines. Disciplinary differences may also reveal differences in reference groups. Thus, this chapter asks: To what extent does the use of the university as a reference group differ by employment status, degree attainment, and academic discipline? Moreover, how have these differences changed over the last twenty-five years?

NEW DIRECTIONS FOR COMMUNITY COLLEGES, no. 118, Summer 2002 © Wiley Periodicals, Inc.

21

Review of the Literature

Cohen and Brawer (1977) indicate an increased tendency for community college faculty to list the university as the primary reference group and to view favorably the possibility of working at the university. However, when asked to rate sources of teaching advice, university professors are ranked fourth after colleagues, students, and department chairpersons, but before high school teachers. Cohen and Brawer also find notable differences by groups. They report that people with doctorates, part-time instructors, and faculty in the humanities fields are more inclined toward the university than are full-time faculty, people without doctorates, and instructors in occupational fields. They explain that those who look most to the university as their reference group tend to work part-time and are oriented to their teaching disciplines, research, and professional preparation. People who refer least to the university tend to be "old timers" with many more years of experience. Because they are less interested in further professional development, Cohen and Brawer speculate, secondary school teachers play a minimal role in the orientation of future community college faculty.

In a study of community college reference groups, Hill and Morrison (1976) also indicate that faculty with lower degrees tend not to identify with the senior institution (which for our purposes can be noted as the four-year college or university). In regard to disciplinary differences, they find that faculty in the humanities and social sciences are inclined toward the university as the stronger reference group, whereas faculty in the vocational fields (education, business, and nursing) are not.

Some explanations for these differences might be provided by the work of Bland (1983). He contends that community college instructors are more concerned with job security and recognition from their superiors than with being committed to the views of their colleagues. He further finds, however, that the judgment of colleagues in their local departments is more important than of colleagues in their disciplines.

These findings shed light on the focus of this chapter: whether they hold true now, decades after they were first reported. In addition, whether reference groups differ by employment status and degree attainment are other influential distinctions worthy of investigation. Therefore, this chapter presents findings on faculty reference groups and possible differences by professional background (i.e., full-time/part-time status, earned degree) and teaching realm (i.e., disciplinary field).

Method

The data are derived from the 2000 Community College Faculty Survey. All 1,531 surveyed faculty are included in the analyses. Selected survey questions have been combined to form a "University as a Reference Group"

(URG) composite. For more details on the creation of this and other analytical constructors, see Outcalt, 2002. The reference group construct comprises a series of questions on the degree of interaction with university faculty members, perceptions of university faculty, experience in graduate education, and university goals (scale: 1–40). Means were tested by conducting analyses of variance (ANOVA) level. All reported means and differences are statistically significant at the .05 level unless reported otherwise.

University as a Reference Group

The following section describes whether respondents' overall scores on the URG construct differ by respondent part-time/full-time status, degree attainment, and degree earned. The results presented here both support and challenge previous findings.

Differences by Background Characteristics. Overall, community college faculty are influenced by the university. Contrary to what was earlier reported by Cohen and Brawer (1977), part-time faculty no longer affiliate themselves more with the university than do full-time faculty. The lack of a statistically significant difference, however, does not mean the forms of university influence are the same for both part-time and full-time faculty. As suggested later in this chapter, many part-time faculty aspire to teach at the university. Particularly given the surplus of trained college instructors and limited positions in the four-year college and university, the community college may serve as a temporary (and part-time) position for many. For different reasons, full-time faculty may also identify with the university given their tenure status and educational attainment. Nonetheless, the degree to which the university serves as a reference group is relatively similar for both part-time and full-time faculty.

Similarly, in regard to their use of reference groups, faculty who hold doctorates do not differ from those who do not. Although twenty-five years ago Hill and Morrison (1976) found more identification with the university among those with lower degrees, there appears to be no significant difference today.

Differences by Teaching Realm. When grouped by teaching discipline, faculty reflect varying degrees of identification with the university as a reference group. Disciplines are categorized according to primary teaching field (Outcalt, 2002). The major significant difference uncovered in this study is that faculty in math and computer sciences report weaker identification with the university than do faculty in the humanities, English, fine arts, sciences, and social sciences. This is similar to Hill and Morrison's finding (1976) that faculty in the humanities and social sciences are inclined toward the university as the stronger reference group. (This chapter follows the disciplinary classification scheme employed by Cohen and Brawer

[1977].) For many, courses in the majority of these fields may be equivalent (and therefore transferable) to university introduction courses. Students who participate in these classes may also aspire to continue their education at the university level. Conversely, faculty in the technical and vocational programs, as reflected by the math and computer sciences fields, identify themselves less with the four-year college. These programs may grant terminal degrees at the community college and are not usually intended to advance to the university level.

Because the URG comprised many elements, opinions, and behaviors, the following sections will examine specific dimensions of the reference group and how they differ by teaching background and discipline.

Sources of Teaching Advice

One key question within the URG was the extent to which university professors are viewed by respondents as useful sources of advice on teaching. Overall, community college faculty rate university professors as "somewhat useful" (1.81) (Scale: 3 = quite useful, 2 = somewhat useful, 1 = not very useful). High school teachers are rated as less useful (1.59) than university professors. This finding demonstrates that the university is a stronger source of influence in regard to teaching. These rankings are somewhat similar to the findings of Cohen and Brawer (1977). However, professional journals and professional organization programs are ranked higher (2.14 and 2.10, respectively) than university professors, whereas university professors are rated higher than professional journals and programs in the 1975 study. This unexpected finding indicates an increased tendency to refer to professional groups, which may serve as an extension of university professors as sources of teaching advice.

Differences by Background Characteristics. Significant differences exist between teaching backgrounds and fields. Full-timers and part-timers differ in the extent to which they rate university professors as useful sources of teaching advice. Full-time faculty report university professors to be less useful (1.78) than do part-time faculty (1.89) (scale: 3 = quite useful, 2 = somewhat useful, 1 = not very useful). Two possible reasons are that full-time faculty, given their greater experience, may not actively seek teaching advice as would part-time faculty, and that part-time faculty may have recently attended a university and would thereby favorably refer to those they have most recently observed and experienced (Cohen and Brawer, 1977). Interestingly, part-time faculty also rate high school teachers as more useful (1.61) than full-time faculty (1.58). Again, part-time faculty may still be "in training" or be high school teachers working part-time at the community college and thus encounter more sources of teaching than full-time faculty. Overall, both groups rate university professors favorably, although differences do exist between full-time and part-time faculty. Moreover, these differences are a function of their full-time and part-time status and are not related to any significant differences in whether they hold doctorate degrees.

Differences by Teaching Realm. Distinct disciplinary differences also exist concerning sources of advice on teaching. Faculty in the humanities rate university professors as more useful than do faculty in math and computer sciences (1.99 and 1.73, respectively). Moreover, faculty in the sciences and math and computer sciences rate high school teachers as more useful than do faculty in the social sciences (1.73, 1.69, and 1.38, respectively). These differences may be attributable to the transferability of courses within these fields.

Other Dimensions of the Reference Group

Overall, the university remains a significant reference group for community college faculty. For the most part, few significant differences exist with respect to the other dimensions of the reference group (career aspirations, community college function, student referral, and contact with university faculty). Table 2.1 summarizes the significant differences by background characteristics and teaching field.

Aspiring to Future Faculty Positions. According to Table 2.1, about half the faculty is attracted to a university position, part-time faculty more so than full-time faculty. The exact reasons, however, are unclear. Some part-time faculty may be more attracted to the university simply because of the opportunity to find full-time work. Other part-time faculty may view

Table 2.1. Significant Differences Across Dimensions of the University as a Reference Group

Characteristics	N	Future University Position	Refer Students to University Resources	Closer Contact with University Faculty
Part-Time	467	1.59	—	—
Full-Time	1064	1.45	—	—
Ph.D. Degree	239	1.61	—	—
English	178	—	1.74	—
Humanities	200	—	1.76	—
Math/Comp. Sci.	179	—	1.59	—
Science	131	—	—	—
Social Science	105	—	1.77	—
Overall	1531	1.49	1.70	1.81

Note: Nonsignificant mean differences are not included.

"Future Faculty Position" Scale: 1–2 (1 = Unattractive; 2 = Attractive)

"Refer Students to University Resources" Scale: 1–2 (1 = No; 2 = Yes)

"Closer Contact with Faculty" Scale: 1–2 (1 = No; 2 = Yes)

Table 2.2. Community College Function Rankings

Function	Mean Ranking	Standard Deviation
New Job Entry Skills	2.27	1.48
Prebaccalaureate Transfer	2.35	1.67
Career Skills Upgrading	2.76	1.38
Lifelong Learning	3.37	1.91
Remedial Education	3.73	1.88
Community Development	4.49	1.78

Note: N = 1258

Scale: 1–6 (1 = most important, 2 = second most important, 3 = third most important, etc.)

their current positions as a step toward university teaching. Additional findings further indicate that those holding a doctorate degree are more likely to aspire (and to qualify) to teach in the university setting than those without an advanced degree. Interestingly, with respect to future university faculty aspirations, no disciplinary differences appear to exist.

Referring Students to University Resources. When asked about resources at the university, the majority of the sample indicate that they would suggest that their students make use of university resources. No teaching background differences are present, although disciplinary differences do exist. Humanities, social sciences, and English faculty refer more often to the university than math and computer sciences faculty.

Closer Contact with Faculty. Over 80 percent of the community college faculty report that they would prefer more frequent contact with university faculty. There are no significant differences, however, by part-time/full-time status, degree attainment, and disciplinary field. In other words, community college faculty, as a whole, would enjoy communication with university professors, but no one particular subgroup of community college faculty desires more or less contact.

Community College Function. Overall, training students to enter new jobs shows the highest mean ranking among the functions of the community college (Table 2.2), followed by baccalaureate transfer, upgrading career skills, lifelong learning, and remedial education. Community development ranks last among the list of community college functions. Based on these results, community college faculty, overall, prioritize the student outcomes (i.e., career skills and transfer) that often distinguish the two-year from the four-year college. No significant differences by faculty characteristics exist regarding the transfer function of the community college.

Discussion

This chapter reexamines the extent to which the university serves as an important source of identification for community college faculty, as predicted by Cohen and Brawer (1977) twenty-five years ago. Although the results indicate that the university remains an influential reference group for today's community college faculty, perceptions by various groups have changed over time. Most notably, part-time faculty no longer indicate greater identification with the university than do full-time faculty. Rather, there is hardly a difference in their overall identification with university professors. Moreover, part-time faculty consider high school teachers as *more useful* sources of teaching than university faculty. Perhaps high school teachers have received higher ratings because they have become more visible to part-time community college faculty. Conversely, university faculty may be less available, as a great majority of community college faculty report that they would enjoy more interactions with university faculty.

For many community college faculty, university teaching continues to be an appealing future occupation, supporting previous claims that for some, positions at the community college serve as a temporary step toward a faculty position in a four-year college or university. Faculty with doctorates report being most attracted to working at a university. However, an alternative explanation can be made that the appeal of working for a university may not necessarily be a "higher" step in one's professorial occupation but rather serve as an alternative to working part-time. Especially given the growing percentage of part-time community college faculty at a number of institutions nationwide, part-time faculty may be in a continual state of looking for greater job stability.

Previous research has offered some insights into differences in the use of reference groups according to respondent backgrounds; disciplinary differences also play a significant role in understanding reference groups. Liberal arts faculty, for example, tend to refer more often to the university as a source of advice than do those in the math and computer sciences fields. More than likely, the courses in the humanities and social sciences, in particular, are meant to offer prebaccalaureate transfer credit. While some math and computer sciences courses are also transferable, some courses in these fields also include vocational studies. For this reason, the university does not play as influential a role for this group.

The findings presented here have implications for both research and practice. First, the community colleges are trying to fulfill a variety of needs, from prebaccalaureate transfer preparation to job training to community development. This multiplicity of needs has a bearing on reference group identification. Given the numerous goals within a single community college, one must examine the community college from multiple dimensions. Besides disciplinary differences, major differences also exist with regard to teaching background (part-time/full-time and degree attainment). Second, different resources should be made available for these distinct groups. Both university and secondary school information should be accessible to different faculty for different needs. Given that part-time faculty constitute an increasing proportion of the community college faculty population, instructional resources as well as employment security and benefits (as would be provided for full-time faculty) should especially be made available for this neglected and often transient group. Part-time faculty may have their own distinct set of values and assumptions, which should be recognized and addressed by the institution. Related future studies should continue to examine distinctions within the part-time faculty population and how to best meet their specific needs.

References

Bland, W. D. "Role Orientations and Evaluation of Professional Performance." *Community College Review,* 1983, *10*(2), 27–32.

Cohen, A. M., and Brawer, F. B. *The Two-Year College Instructor Today.* New York: Praeger, 1977.

Hill, M., and Morrison, J. "The Relationship of Selected Community College Faculty Attitudes, Socialization Experiences, and Reference Group Identities." *Community/Junior College Research Quarterly,* 1976, *1,* 25–50.

Outcalt, C. "A Profile of the Community College Professoriate, 1975–2000." Unpublished doctoral dissertation, Graduate School of Education and Information Studies, University of California-Los Angeles, 2002.

Seidman, E. *In the Words of the Faculty: Perspectives on Improving Teaching and Educational Quality in Community Colleges.* San Francisco: Jossey-Bass, 1985.

JENNY J. LEE is a doctoral student in the Graduate School of Education and Information Studies at the University of California–Los Angeles and a research analyst at the Higher Education Research Institute.

PART TWO

The Heart of Professional Practice: Teaching and Student Interaction

Critically reflective teaching asks community college teachers to discover and research the assumptions they make about teaching and learning by using the four lenses available to them: students' eyes, colleagues' perceptions, educational literature, and teachers' autobiographical experiences as learners. Viewing classroom practice through these four lenses helps teachers make more informed judgments and take more informed actions, in community college classrooms.

3

Using the Lenses of Critically Reflective Teaching in the Community College Classroom

Stephen D. Brookfield

Community college classrooms represent the ultimate in open-entry admissions in American higher education. Characterized by student diversity in all its facets—racial, gender, and socioeconomic as well as by wide differences in ability, educational readiness, motivation, and age—the community college classroom is a varied and sometimes volatile mix. A critically reflective stance toward the practice of community college teaching can help teachers feel more confident that their judgments are informed and leave them with energy and intent to do good work.

This chapter explores the idea of critical reflection as it is informed by the literature of reflective teaching in general and by two subcategories of this literature in particular–teacher decision making and classroom assessment. A frequently mentioned premise of reflective practice is that it helps teachers make more informed decisions (Valli, 1993; Calderhead and Gates, 1993; Brubacher, Case, and Reagan, 1994). If teachers are more reflective, the argument goes, they will be better placed to make good judgments about appropriate instructional approaches, accurate evaluative criteria, helpful curricular sequencing, and useful responses to group problems and other matters. Therefore, informed decision making can be considered the heart of good teaching. The literature on teacher thinking and decision making (Day, Calderhead, and Denicolo, 1993; Day, Pope, and Denicolo, 1990; Carlgren, Handal, and Vaage, 1994) supports this contention, emphasizing the importance of teachers checking their assumptions about good practice against the insights gleaned from colleagues. The literature on classroom research and assessment provides a wealth of examples of how information gained from students concerning their learning can help teachers ground their actions in an informed understanding of a particular classroom's dynamics (Angelo, 1998; Brookhart, 2000). As well as examining how colleagues' perceptions and students' opinions can help teachers unearth and challenge their assumptions, this chapter will explore how teachers' autobiographical experiences as learners and their reading of educational theory can help them view their practice from different, and helpful, angles.

Advocates of reflective practice are interested in helping teachers understand, question, investigate, and take seriously their own learning and practice. They argue that professional education has taken a wrong turn in seeing the role of practitioner as interpreter, translator, and implementer of theory produced by academic thinkers and researchers. They believe instead that practitioners develop their own contextually sensitive theories of practice rather than importing them from outside. Work on teachers' personal theorizing (Ross, Cornett, and McCutcheon, 1992; Tann, 1993) describes how reflective teachers are engaged in a continual investigation and monitoring of their efforts. In Smyth's (1992) words, they "perceive themselves as 'active' learners, inquirers and advocates of their own practices, . . . critical theoreticians in their own teaching and the structures in which they are located" (p. 32).

Teaching in a critically reflective way involves teachers trying to discover, and research, the assumptions that frame how they teach. In researching these assumptions, teachers have four complementary lenses through which they can view their practice; the lens of their own autobiographies as learners, the lens of students' eyes, the lens of colleagues' perceptions, and the lens of educational literature. Reviewing practice through these lenses helps surface the assumptions we hold about pedagogic methods, techniques, and approaches and the assumptions we make concerning the conditions that best foster student learning. But critical reflection also forces us to confront deeper assumptions concerning the submerged and unacknowledged power dynamics that infuse all practice settings. It also helps us detect hegemonic assumptions—assumptions that we think are in our own best interests but that actually work against us in the long term.

Critically Reflective Lens One: Autobiographical Experiences of Learning

As case studies of beginning and experienced teachers have shown (Bullough, Knowles, and Crow, 1992; Berman and others, 1991; Dollase, 1992), much of how teachers teach is in direct response to how they learned. They try to avoid reproducing the humiliations that they felt were visited upon them as learners and they seek to replicate the things their own teachers did that affirmed or inspired them. One teacher (Knowles, 1993) sums up this autobiographical connection as follows:

As I tried on various roles as a young beginning teacher there were certain cloaks of practice that did not match the rest of my attire—they did not jibe with the kinds of experiences I knew to be most valuable to *me* as a student— and I tended to dismiss them as being not appropriate for the wardrobe of my teaching repertoire. On deeper examination, in some cases, the particular practices in question were connected to approaches or experiences with which or through which I had suffered (such as at the hands of an unethical teacher) or which were associated with punishment or fear of failure (p. 75).

The insights and meanings for practice drawn from experiences of learning are likely to have a profound and long-lasting influence. Teachers may think they are teaching according to a widely accepted curricular or pedagogic model only to find, on reflection, that the foundations of how they work have been laid in their autobiographies as learners. As Day, Denicolo, and Pope (1990) note, when teachers are asked to explain why they favor certain approaches, "frequently they evidence their choice of method, for instance, by reference to a formative experience of their own, whether it be a positive one which they seek to emulate for their students or a negative one which they strive to avoid reiterating for others" (p. 156). A good example of how an experience of learning frames a teacher's life is Andresen's (1993) examination of his own pedagogy. Remembering the joy he felt as a science student at discovering that the physical world could be explained and manipulated, he came to understand his career as a teacher "as a search, a pilgrimage, toward recapturing this primary joy" (p. 62). Clearly, then, studying autobiographical experiences of learning can help explain to teachers why they gravitate to certain ways of working and instinctively turn away from others.

Critically Reflective Lens Two: Learners' Eyes

Seeing yourself through learners' eyes constitutes one of the most consistently surprising elements in any community college teacher's career. In recent years the literature on classroom assessment and classroom research has explored this process and provided numerous suggestions for techniques such as "the muddiest point" and the "one minute paper" that have become popular among many instructors (Angelo, 1998). At the heart of classroom research is the belief that informed decision making depends on teachers' having accurate information regarding how and what students are learning. Whenever teachers use some form of classroom assessment to find out how their students are experiencing the class, they learn something. As Hammersley (1986, 1993) documents, sometimes what they find is reassuring. They discover that learners are interpreting their actions in the way they are intended to or that students are roughly at the point in their understanding of subject matter that teachers believe them to be.

But often teachers are profoundly surprised by the diversity of meanings people read into their words and actions or by the spread of abilities and levels of student comprehension revealed.

Seeing their practice through learners' eyes helps teachers teach more responsively. Having a sense of what is happening to students as they grapple with the difficult, threatening, and exhilarating process of learning constitutes instructors' primary pedagogic information. Without this information it is hard to teach well. It is obviously important to have a good grasp of methods, but it is just as important to gain some regular insight into what is happening to learners as those methods are put into practice. Without an appreciation of how people are experiencing learning, any methodological choices we make risk being ill informed, inappropriate, or harmful.

Critically Reflective Lens Three: Our Colleagues' Experiences

In their study of the social realities of teaching, Lieberman and Miller (1991) note that among teachers "there is a general lack of confidence, a pervasive feeling of vulnerability, a fear of being 'found out.' Such feelings are made worse because of the privacy ethic. There is no safe place to air one's uncertainties and to get the kind of feedback necessary to reduce the anxiety about being a good teacher, or at least an adequate one" (p. 103). One way to counter this isolation is through teacher reflection groups (Hauser, 1994), "talking teaching" groups (Clark, 2001), and conversation circles on pedagogy (Collay, Dunlap, Enloe, and Gagnon, 1998). In these groups teachers use one another as critical mirrors and sounding boards, providing them with images and interpretations of their practice that often take them by surprise. By reviewing experiences dealing with the same crises and dilemmas they face, teachers can check, reframe, and broaden their own theories of practice. Case studies of teacher reflection groups (Berkey and others, 1990; Miller, 1990; Osterman and Kottkamp, 1993) report that talking to colleagues about problems they have in common increases teachers' chances of stumbling across interpretations that fit what is happening in a particular situation.

Just as important as checking readings of problems, responses, assumptions, and justifications against the readings offered by colleagues is the emotional sustenance such conversation provides. According to participants in the studies mentioned above, teachers start to realize that what they thought were unique problems and idiosyncratic failings are shared by many others who work in situations like theirs. Just knowing that they are not alone in their struggles can, as Berlak and Berlak (1981) show, relieve teachers of unwarranted feelings of incompetence. So although critical reflection often begins alone, it is most fruitfully conducted as a collective endeavor. Teachers need colleagues to help them know what their assumptions are, how these could be researched, and how they might change their practices.

Critically Reflective Lens Four: Theoretical Literature

Theory can help teachers "name" their practice by illuminating the general elements of what they think are idiosyncratic experiences. It can provide multiple perspectives on familiar situations. In particular, studying theory can help teachers combat the sense of impostorship that frequently troubles their existence. As told by teachers themselves, impostorship is the sense teachers possess that they do not really deserve to be taken seriously as competent professionals because they know they do not really know what they're doing. All they are certain of is that unless they are very careful, they will be found out to be teaching under false pretences. Elbaz (1987) notes that teachers who feel like impostors have a destructive tendency to accept all the blame for failure in a particular situation. Sometimes teachers' feelings of impostorship are communicated to students, inducing in them an unnecessary anxiety and level of mistrust or doubt. For example, Brems, Baldwin, Davis, and Namyniuk (1994) report that teachers with self-reported feelings of impostorship are viewed less favorably by students.

One effect of impostorship is that teachers who feel it are reluctant to ask for assistance. As Clark (1992) comments, "Asking for help makes us feel vulnerable—vulnerable to being discovered as imposters who don't know as much as we pretend to know" (p. 82). For those teachers unable to approach colleagues for aid, a text can be a useful substitute. Educational literature can provide teachers with an analysis of dilemmas and problematic situations that can be enormously helpful. In her study of classroom chronicles, Isenberg (1994) shows how reading others' depictions of the crises, anxieties, and dilemmas that she thought were uniquely her own helped her put her own problems in perspective. The burgeoning literature on how teachers can learn from reading narratives of teaching (Jalongo and Isenberg, 1995; Preskill and Jacobwitz, 2001) shows that this activity can help teachers realize that what they thought were signs of their personal failings as practitioners are sometimes situations that were externally created and over which they have little control. This stops them from falling victim to the belief that they are responsible for everything that happens in their classrooms.

This belief is vividly documented in Britzman's (1991) study of beginning teachers. Britzman records how "because they took on the myth that everything depends on the teacher, when things went awry, all they could do was blame themselves rather than reflect upon the complexity of pedagogical encounters" (p. 227). Teachers who subscribe to this myth often assume that student lassitude or hostility is the result of teachers not being enthusiastic enough. They believe they have failed to use the right pedagogical approaches, or that they have not been sufficiently creative in finding points of connection between the subject matter they teach and their students' lives. It can be an important act of critical reflection for teachers to read a theoretical analysis that helps them to switch their interpretive frame so that they view the reasons for students' apathy or anger differently. Theories of cognitive and developmental psychology suggest that when learners realize that they are on the verge of changing, or scrutinizing, aspects of their thinking that they would prefer to leave untouched, the fear and resentment this produces are directed at teachers (Perry, 1988; Basseches, 1984; King and Kitchener, 1994; Ignelzi, 2000).

Conclusion

This chapter has drawn on the literature of reflective practice, teacher thinking, and classroom research to argue that critical reflection is important to community college teachers' mental health and professional competence. Researchers argue that being critically reflective helps teachers make informed decisions in the classroom. It helps them distinguish the dimensions of students' actions and motivations they can affect from those that are beyond their influence. It also helps them develop a rationale for their practice that they can call on to guide them in making difficult decisions in unpredictable situations. As work on classroom research demonstrates, checking teachers' assumptions about teaching practices against students' perceptions of those same practices can alert them to those assumptions they can depend on and those they need to reframe.

Methods that have been documented as helpful to community college teachers' critical reflection include classroom critical-incident questionnaires, student-learning audits, teacher-assumption inventories, protocols of critical conversation, selective reading in the literature of teachers' stories, teacher portfolios, and teachers placing themselves in the role of learners (Brookfield, 1995). The interviews cited earlier with teachers engaged in critical-reflection groups and the research into teacher thinking (also previously cited) both document how instructors view a set of critically examined core assumptions as a survival necessity. Surfacing and examining the assumptions that frame the decisions they make in the classroom give community college teachers a greater sense of confidence in the accuracy of those choices. If asked by students or colleagues to explain the particularities of their actions, teachers can give a rationale that induces in those same students or colleagues the reassuring sense that these teachers have an examined justification for why they do what they do. Teachers also comment that the surprise, shock, and productive uncertainty occasioned by critical reflection reenergizes their sense of engagement in practice. For teachers in mid- or late career this is an important, and unlooked-for, benefit. Finally, students report that seeing their teachers talk out loud about how critical reflection is confirming or challenging their pedagogic assumptions models for those same students the process of critical thinking.

In community college settings—perhaps the ultimate in diverse, open-entry, mixed-ability classrooms—critical reflection on core assumptions can ground teachers in a moral, intellectual, and political vision of what they are trying to accomplish.

References

Andresen, L. "On Becoming a Maker of Teachers: Journey Down a Long Hall of Mirrors." In D. Boud, R. Cohen, and D. Walker (eds.), *Using Experience for Learning*. Bristol, Pa.: The Open University Press, 1993.

Angelo, T.A. (ed.). *Classroom Assessment and Research: An Update on Uses, Approaches, and Research Findings*. New Directions for Teaching and Learning, no. 75. San Francisco: Jossey-Bass, 1998.

Basseches, M. *Dialectical Thinking and Adult Development*. Norwood, N.J.: Ablex, 1984.

Berkey, R., and others. "Collaborating for Reflective Practice: Voices of Teachers, Administrators, and Researchers." In *Education and Urban Society*, 1990, 22(2), 204–232.

Berlak, A., and Berlak, H. *Dilemmas of Schooling: Teaching and Social Change*. New York: Methuen, 1981.

Berman, L. M., and others. *Toward Curriculum for Being: Voices of Educators*. Albany: State University of New York Press, 1991.

Brems, C., Baldwin, M. R., Davis, L., and Namyniuk, L. "The Imposter Syndrome as Related to Teaching Evaluations and Advising Relationships of University Teachers." *Journal of Higher Education*, 1994, 65(2), 183–193.

Britzman, D. P. *Practice Makes Practice: A Critical Study of Learning to Teach*. Albany: State University of New York Press, 1991.

Brookfield, S. D. *Becoming a Critically Reflective Teacher*. San Francisco: Jossey-Bass, 1995.

Brookhart, S. M. *The Art and Science of Classroom Assessment: The Missing Part of Pedagogy*. ASHE-ERIC Higher Education Report, 27(1). San Francisco: Jossey-Bass, 2000.

Brubacher, J. W., Case, C. W., and Reagan, T. G. *Becoming a Reflective Educator: How to Build a Culture of Inquiry in the Schools*. Thousand Oaks, Calif.: Corwin Press, 1994.

Bullough, R. V., Knowles, J. G., and Crow, N. A. *Emerging as a Teacher*. New York: Routledge, 1992.

Calderhead, J., and Gates, P. (eds.). *Conceptualizing Reflection in Teacher Development*. Bristol, Pa.: Falmer Press, 1993.

Carlgren, I., Handal, G., and Vaage, S. (eds.). *Teachers' Minds and Actions: Research on Teachers' Thinking and Practice*. Bristol, Pa.: Falmer Press, 1994.

Clark, C. M. "Teachers as Designers in Self-Directed Development." In A. Hargreaves and M. G. Fullan (eds.), *Understanding Teacher Development*. New York: Teachers College Press, 1992.

Clark, C. M. *Talking Shop: Authentic Conversation and Teacher Learning*. New York: Teachers College Press, 2001.

Collay, M., Dunlap, D., Enloe, W., and Gagnon, G. W. *Learning Circles: Creating Conditions for Professional Development*. Thousand Oaks, Calif.: Corwin Press, 1998.

Day, C., Calderhead, J., and Denicolo, P. (eds.). *Research on Teacher Thinking: Understanding Professional Development*, Bristol, Pa.: Falmer Press, 1993.

Day, C., Pope, M., and Denicolo, M. (eds.). *Insight into Teachers' Thinking and Practice*. Bristol, Pa.: Falmer Press, 1990.

Dollase, R. H. *Voices of Beginning Teachers*. New York: Teachers College Press, 1992.

Elbaz, F. "Teachers' Knowledge of Teaching: Strategies for Reflection." In J. Smyth (ed.), *Educating Teachers: Changing the Nature of Pedagogical Knowledge*. Philadelphia: Falmer Press, 1987.

Hammersley, M. *Case Studies in Classroom Research*. Bristol, Pa.: Open University Press, 1986.

Hammersley, M. (ed.). *Controversies in Classroom Research.* Bristol, Pa.: Open University Press, 1993.

Hauser, M. E. "Working with School Staff: Reflective Cultural Analysis in Groups." In G. D. Spindler and L. Spindler (eds.), *Pathways to Cultural Awareness: Cultural Therapy with Teachers and Students.* Thousand Oaks, Calif.: Corwin, 1994.

Ignelzi, M. "Meaning-Making in the Learning and Teaching Process." In M. B. Baxter Magolda (ed.), *Teaching to Promote Intellectual and Personal Maturity: Incorporating Students' Worldviews and Identities into the Learning Process.* New Directions for Teaching and Learning, no. 82. San Francisco: Jossey-Bass, 2000.

Isenberg, J. *Going by the Book: The Role of Popular Classroom Chronicles in the Professional Development of Teachers.* New York: Routledge, 1994.

Jalongo, M. R., and Isenberg, J. P. *Teachers' Stories: From Personal Narrative to Professional Insight.* San Francisco: Jossey-Bass, 1995.

King, P. M., and Kitchener, K. S. *Developing Reflective Judgment: Understanding and Promoting Intellectual Growth and Critical Thinking in Adolescents and Adults.* San Francisco: Jossey-Bass, 1994.

Knowles, J. G. "Life-History Accounts as Mirrors: A Practical Avenue for the Conceptualization of Reflection in Teacher Education." In J. Calderhead and P. Gates (eds.), *Conceptualizing Reflection in Teacher Development.* Bristol, Pa.: Falmer Press, 1993.

Lieberman, A., and Miller, L. (eds.). *Staff Development for Education in the '90s: New Demands, New Realities, New Perspectives.* New York: Teachers College Press, 1991.

Miller, J. L. *Creating Spaces and Finding Voices: Teachers Collaborating for Empowerment.* Albany: State University of New York Press, 1990.

Osterman, K. F., and Kottkamp, R. B. *Reflective Practice for Educators: Improving Schooling through Professional Development.* Newbury Park, Calif.: Corwin Press, 1993.

Perry, W. G. "Different Worlds in the Same Classroom." In P. Ramsden (ed.), *Improving Learning: New Perspectives.* New York: Nichols, 1988.

Preskill, S. L., and Jacobwitz, R. S. *Stories of Teaching.* Upper Saddle River, N.J.: Prentice Hall, 2001

Ross, D., Cornett, J., and McCutcheon, G. (eds.). *Teachers' Personal Theorizing.* Albany: State University of New York Press, 1992.

Smyth, J. "Teachers' Work and the Politics of Reflection." *American Educational Research Journal,* 1992, *29*(2), 267–300.

Tann, S. "Eliciting Student Teachers' Personal Theories." In J. Calderhead and P. Gates (eds.), *Conceptualizing Reflection in Teacher Development.* Bristol, Pa.: Falmer Press, 1993, 53–69.

Valli, L. (ed.). *Reflective Teacher Education: Cases and Critiques.* Albany: State University of New York Press, 1993.

STEPHEN D. BROOKFIELD *holds the title of distinguished professor at the University of St. Thomas in Minneapolis. He is currently a visiting professor at Harvard University, Graduate School of Education.*

Exploring differences between instructional practices of full-time and part-time faculty, this chapter reveals that the average time spent by part- and full-time faculty in most classroom instructional practices is essentially equivalent. However, differences emerge regarding time spent in various classroom practices, the availability of faculty to students outside class, and faculty connections with colleagues and the institution.

Instructional Practices of Part-Time and Full-Time Faculty

Pam Schuetz

Although the trend toward increasing dependence upon part-time faculty in community colleges is clearly documented, the question remains whether greater use of part-time faculty undermines or contributes to teaching effectiveness and student learning (Cohen and Brawer, 1996; Friedlander, 1980; Grubb and others, 1999). Previous studies of part-time and full-time faculty at community colleges have generated mixed results. Some cite little or no differences in terms of instructional practices or teaching skills (Gappa and Leslie, 1993; Roueche, Roueche, and Milliron, 1996), while others indicate clear differences (Digranes and Digranes, 1995; Thompson, 1992). After a review of ERIC documents, Banachowski (1996) surmises that "studies to support the contention that part-timers are less (or for that matter more) effective teachers than full-timers are inconclusive" (p. 58). These contradictory findings suggest that the issue is complex and further investigation is warranted.

Pascarella and Terenzini (1991) assert that "although it may be overstated to say that we know what causes effective teaching, we do know much about what effective teachers do and how they behave in their classroom" (p. 110). Using results of a recent faculty survey, the purpose of this chapter is to test the hypothesis that part-time and full-time community college faculty "do and behave" in essentially equivalent ways with respect to two types of instructional practices.

Method

This analysis is based on the 2000 Center for the Study of Community Colleges (CSCC) survey of more than 1,500 faculty respondents from over one hundred community colleges nationwide (see "Editor's Notes" for a detailed description of the 2000 CSCC survey). Of the respondents, 424 (29 percent) were part-time faculty and 1,062 (71 percent) were full-time. Though full-time faculty are overrepresented in this sample, the proportion of part-time and full-time faculty in the sample is similar to national norms on the proportion of instructional hours each group teaches (U.S. Department of Education, 2000). (Part-timers are defined as those who did not answer yes to either of the following survey questions: "Are you considered a full-time faculty member at this college?" or "Are you considered a full-time faculty member elsewhere?") Forty-six (3 percent) of the original sample of 1,532 faculty did not respond to the question of employment status, and were therefore excluded from the following analysis. Cross-tabulations, chi-square statistics, t-tests for independent samples comparing group means, and tests of proportions (Agresti and Finlay, 1997) were used to identify statistically significant similarities and differences between part-time and full-time faculty responses to questions describing instructional practices. Figures cited in this chapter for comparison of part-time and full-time faculty are all statistically significant at $p<0.05$.

Instructional Practices

In a broad sense, instructional practices may be defined as faculty behaviors that help students learn. Given the scope of CSCC survey questions, this chapter will focus on two types of instructional practices: (1) teaching methods (ways of presenting instructional materials or conducting instructional activities) and (2) faculty behaviors outside of the classroom that directly or closely support student learning, including interactions with students, colleagues, and the institution.

Teaching Methods. Respondents were asked to estimate the percentage of class time spent on the following instructional activities: faculty's own lectures, guest lecturers, students' verbal presentations, class discussion, viewing or listening to films and taped media, simulation and gaming, quizzes and examinations, field trips, lecture and demonstration experiments, laboratory experiments by students, laboratory practical examinations and quizzes, student use of computers and the Internet, and other (respondents were asked to specify).

Group means for part-time ($N=424$) and full-time faculty ($N=1,062$) responses indicate very similar use of class time regardless of faculty employment status. Each group uses an average of 43 percent of class time for lectures, 15 percent for class discussions, and 11 percent for quizzes and examinations, accounting for over two-thirds of class time with these three teaching methods alone. Most of the remaining third of class time is split among student use of computers/Internet (7 percent), student verbal presentations (5 percent), viewing and/or listening to films or taped media (4 percent), other (4 percent), simulation/gaming (2 percent), and field trips

(1 percent). There is only one instructional practice—the average percentage of class time spent in "laboratory experiments by students"—where part-time faculty response (4 percent) is statistically distinguishable from full-time faculty response (7 percent).

If group means were the only measure examined, part-time and full-time faculty use of class time would be virtually indistinguishable. This finding is in keeping with other studies describing average faculty use of class time by employment status, including a recent national report (U.S. Department of Education, 2001). However, significant differences between part- and full-time instructional practices do emerge when the distribution of the data rather than group means is examined.

A number of statistically significant differences between part-time and full-time instructional practices emerge from considering what faculty members tend never to do. For example, more part-time faculty never use guest lecturers (75 percent of part-timers vs. 69 percent of full-timers), films or taped media (49 percent vs. 40 percent), or laboratory experiments by students (80 percent vs. 69 percent) or encourage student use of computers or the Internet (61 percent vs. 49 percent) during class. Therefore, students enrolled in classes taught by part-timers would be less likely to experience these kinds of instructional practices on average than students enrolled in full-timers' classes. While most of these differences "wash out" when expressed as group means, cross-tabulations suggest a direction for future study in differentiating between the instructional practices of some part-time and full-time faculty.

Another difference between part- and full-time faculty emerges from unpacking "other" instructional responses. Fifteen percent of part-time and 16 percent of full-time respondents specify an "other" instructional activity in addition to the twelve specific options listed in the survey. While admittedly little class time is devoted to these "other" instructional practices, it is interesting to note that full-timers report using collaboration techniques, group activities, and teamwork assignments in the classroom almost three times as often as part-timers (27 percent vs. 10 percent). Since enhanced student learning has been correlated with such collaborative activities, this finding suggests a direction for future research documenting differences between the instructional practices of part-time and full-time faculty (Gappa and Leslie, 1993; Grubb, 1999; Kuh and Vesper, 1997; Tinto, 1993).

Instructional Practices Outside of the Classroom. While many faculty behaviors commonly classified as instructional practices occur in the classroom, there are important exceptions. For example, survey results indicate that part-timers are less likely to have revised their syllabus or teaching objectives in the past three years (87 percent vs. 97 percent), less likely to have prepared a replicable or multimedia instructional program for use in the classroom (42 percent vs. 53 percent), less likely to have ever developed extracurricular activities for students related to their fields (60 percent vs. 74 percent), and less likely to have spent no time planning instruction (21 percent vs. 15 percent) on their most recent working day.

Faculty interaction with students outside class has been cited as important to student learning (Astin, 1993; Kuh and Vesper, 1997; Thompson, 2001; Tinto, 1993). The CSCC survey results indicate that part-time faculty are twice as likely to report spending no time with students outside class (35 percent vs. 16 percent for full-time faculty) on their most recent working day. However, survey results also indicate that part-timers are almost as likely as full-timers (47 percent vs. 52 percent) to have spent an hour with students outside class on their most recent working day–a remarkable effort, as few part-timers have offices or phones or receive compensation for office hours (Grubb, 1999). Are students of part-time faculty at a disadvantage because some of their instructors tend to be less available outside of class? Studies indicate that the effect of faculty-student interactions on student learning may be indirect or dependent upon a complex array of student, faculty, and institutional factors not addressed in the CSCC survey. Further research appears necessary to assess the impact of faculty-student interactions on student learning according to faculty employment status (Astin, 1993; Kuh and Hu, 2001; Pascarella and Terenzini, 1991; Tinto, 1993).

In addition to faculty-student contact, effective instructional practices have been shown to be related to faculty interaction with their colleagues and institutions (Grubb, 1999).

> Good teachers were likely to be strongly connected with other faculty, even teaching jointly while ineffective teachers were generally alienated from their peers. . . . In many departments, a large number of part-time instructors slip in and out of their classrooms without much interaction with the rest of the institution. They are hired casually, and rarely are they reviewed by other faculty. . . . Without contact among colleagues, there are few discussions about instruction, no forums where the special pedagogical problems of community college can be debated and resolved, and no ways to bring problems to the attention of administrators (pp. 55, 334).

Overall, it appears that the average behavior of part-time and full-time instructors on their most recent working day indicates several differences with respect to their involvement with their colleagues and institution. For instance, more part-time than full-time faculty report no interaction with colleagues on their most recent working day (48 percent vs. 25 percent of full-timers). Part-timers are less likely to have taught courses jointly with faculty members outside of their department (16 percent vs. 24 percent), and more likely to have spent no time on administrative activities including committee work (66 percent vs. 32 percent) on their most recent working day. These findings suggest a relative isolation of part-timers from colleagues and administrative activities, which in turn suggests isolation from knowledge about innovative teaching methods and campus services from which they and their students might benefit. Indeed, part-timers report less awareness of student needs or campus support services than full-timers, with 34 percent (vs. 20 percent of full-timers) indicating that they do not know or have no opinion about whether the college provides or students are taking advantage of counseling and tutorial services.

Given the increasing diversity of the student body and the accelerating rate of technological change, there seems to be no one best teaching style. Effective teaching may depend on the instructor's ability to adapt a range of teaching methods to meet a variety of needs and ends (Adams, 1992; Grubb, 1999). Because graduate education provides few community college instructors with this repertoire of teaching methods (Grubb, 1999; Meyers, Reid and Quina, 1998) and because it has been suggested that faculty who participate in professional development activities tend to use more innovative instructional methods, it seems especially appropriate to examine part-time and full-time faculty use of opportunities for professional development as a measure related to instructional practices (Keim and Biletzky, 1999).

Both full-time and part-time faculty surveyed in this study intend to take advantage of professional development opportunities in the next five years (83 percent and 76 percent). Full-time faculty are more likely to report behaviors indicating that they are following through on these intentions. For example, full-timers are more likely to have joined national or regional nondisciplinary associations (46 percent vs. 26 percent of part-timers), national or regional disciplinary associations (52 percent vs. 32 percent), and community college-specific associations (29 percent vs. 9 percent). Full-timers are also more likely to have attended meetings of their organizations (22 percent vs. 13 percent) or an academic or professional conference in the past three years (89 percent vs. 66 percent). Overall, these figures suggest that part-timers are less connected than full-timers to professional organizations, colleagues, and administrative activities, all of which support and are likely sources of information about effective instructional practices. This relative lack of interaction with professional colleagues may put part-timers at a disadvantage with respect to enhancing their instructional practices over time (Grubb, 1999; Tinto, 1993).

Some of the differences between part-time and full-time responses to survey questions regarding connections to students, colleagues, and institutions may spring from employment status. This is another point of analysis where simply comparing group mean responses may be inadequate. The teaching experience intervals offered to respondents included: "less than one year," "1–4 years," "5–10 years," "11–20 years," and "over 20 years." Thus a group average of experience (except as an interval) is not meaningful. In addition, the average is a measure vulnerable to the effect of outliers. Looking at the frequency of responses in each interval may be more useful: part-timers most often chose "1–4 years" experience whereas full-timers most often chose "11–20 years" experience at the responding institution. Part-time faculty are three times as likely to report less than one year of teaching experience at the responding institution (17 percent vs. 5 percent) and twice as likely to report less than five years' total teaching experience (42 percent vs. 21 percent for full-timers). In addition, part-time faculty members are almost three times as likely to report teaching three hours per week or less at the responding institution (41 percent vs. 14 percent of full-time faculty). Although these figures may not be surprising given the inherent nature of part-time work, it seems apparent that part-time faculty tend to be less experienced overall and spend less time on campus than full-time faculty. Thus part-time faculty may enjoy fewer opportunities to develop the strong connections to students, colleagues, and institution in ways that have been tied to enhanced student learning (Kuh and Vesper, 1997; Grubb, 1999; Tinto, 1993). (See Chapter Six for further information about part-time and full-time faculty teaching experience.)

Conclusions

The primary purpose of this chapter was to test the hypothesis that the teaching methods and extracurricular involvement with students, colleagues, and institutions reported by part-time faculty in the 2000 CSCC survey are statistically indistinguishable from full-time faculty responses. Based on the analysis here, that hypothesis must be rejected. Although average time spent in various classroom instructional practices was found to be essentially the same, other distinctions between part-time and full-time faculty instructional practices have emerged. Specifically, statistically significant differences in results describing the distribution of instructional practices, faculty availability to students, and connection with colleagues and the institution were identified by employment status.

Although part-time faculty are generally well-qualified to perform their duties, and although many colleges are working to orient and integrate them more fully into the college infrastructure, it can be argued that part-timers are more weakly linked to their students, colleagues, and responding institutions than full-timers (Gappa and Leslie, 1993; McGuire, 1993). This analysis confirmed that part-timers tend to have less total teaching experience, teach fewer hours per week at the responding institution, use less innovative or collaborative teaching methods, and interact less with their students, peers, and institutions. Part-timers tend to be less familiar with availability of campus services (such as tutoring and counseling) and express less knowledge of students' need for or use of support services. Part-timers also are less likely to sustain the kind of extracurricular student-faculty interaction that has been linked to enhanced student learning (Kerekes and Huber, 1998; Stanback-Stroud and others, 1996; Stoecker, Pascarella, and Wolfle, 1988). Ultimately it seems that students are unlikely to receive the same quality of instruction from these more tenuously linked faculty (Academic Senate for California Community Colleges, 1996).

Perhaps, as Gappa and Leslie point out, "Quality suffers—not because part-timers cannot teach well, but because the department or the institution becomes less able to carry out the infrastructure work. People simply do not have enough time to maintain themselves, the institution, and the educational process" (p. 103).

The limited range and specificity of questions pertaining to instructional practices included in the CSCC survey instrument and the lack of student outcomes with which to compare the effects on student learning of statistically different instructional practices of part-time and full-time faculty limit the applicability of this study. Recommended directions for further research include expanding the range of instructional practices considered and matching student learning outcomes to part-time and full-time faculty instructional practices.

References

Academic Senate for California Community Colleges. *The Use Of Part-Time Faculty in California Community Colleges: Issues and Impact.* Sacramento, Calif.: California Community Colleges, 1996.

Adams, M. "Cultural Inclusion in the American College Classroom." In L.L.B. Border and N. V. Chism (eds.), *Teaching for Diversity.* New Directions for Teaching And Learning, no. 49. San Francisco: Jossey-Bass. 1992.

Agresti, A., and Finlay, B. *Statistical Methods for the Social Sciences* (Third Edition), pp. 216–220. Englewood Cliffs, N.J.: Prentice Hall, 1997.

Astin, A. W. *What Matters in College: Four Critical Years Revisited.* San Francisco: Jossey-Bass, 1993.

Banachowski, G. "Review of Part-Time Faculty in the Community College." *Community College Review,* 1996, 24(2), 49–62.

Cohen, A. M., and Brawer, F. *The American Community College* (3rd ed.). San Francisco: Jossey-Bass, 1996.

Digranes, J. L., and Digranes, S. H. "Current and Proposed Uses of Technology for Training Part-Time Faculty." *Community College Journal of Research and Practice,* 1995, 19(2), 161–169.

Friedlander, J. "Instructional Practices of Part-Time Faculty." In M. H. Parsons (ed.), *Using Part-Time Faculty Effectively.* New Directions for Community Colleges, no. 30. San Francisco: Jossey-Bass, 1980.

Gappa, J., and Leslie, D. *The Invisible Faculty: Improving the Status of Part-Timers in Higher Education.* San Francisco: Jossey-Bass, 1993.

Grubb, W. N., and others. *Honored But Invisible: An Inside Look at Teaching in Community Colleges.* San Francisco: Jossey-Bass, 1999.

Keim, M. C., and Biletzky, P. E. "Teaching Methods Used by Part-Time Community College Faculty." *Community College Journal of Research and Practice,* 1999, 23(8), 727–737.

Kerekes, J., and Huber, M. T. *Exceptional Teaching in Community Colleges: An Analysis of Nominations for the U.S. Professors of the Year Program, 1995–1997.* Washington, D.C.: Office of Educational Research and Improvement, 1998.

Kuh, G. D., and Hu, S. "The Effects of Student-Faculty Interaction in the 1990s." *Review of Higher Education,* 2001, 24(3), 309–332.

Kuh, G. D., and Vesper, N. "A Comparison of Student Experience with Good Practices in Undergraduate Education Between 1990 and 1994." *Review of Higher Education,* 1997, 21(1), 43–61.

McGuire, J. "Part-Time Faculty: Partners in Excellence." *Leadership Abstracts,* 1993, 6(6).

Meyers, S. A., Reid, P. T., and Quina, K. "Ready or Not, Here We Come: Preparing Psychology Graduate Students for Academic Careers." *Teaching of Psychology,* 1998, 25(2), 124–126.

Pascarella, E. T., and Terenzini, P. T. *How College Affects Students: Findings and Insights from Twenty Years of Research.* San Francisco: Jossey-Bass, 1991.

Roueche, J. E., Roueche, S. D., and Milliron, M. D. "In the Company of Strangers: Addressing the Utilization and Integration of Part-Time Faculty in American Community Colleges." *Community College Journal of Research and Practice,* 1996, 20(2), 105–117.

Stanback-Stroud, R., and others. "The Use of Part-Time Faculty in California Community Colleges: Issues and Impact." Academic Senate for California Community Colleges, 1996. [http://www.academicsenate.cc.ca.us]

Stoecker, J., Pascarella, E., and Wolfle, L. "Persistence in Higher Education: A Nine-Year Test of a Theoretical Model." *Journal of College Student Development,* 1988, 29(3), 196–209.

Thompson, K. "Recognizing Mutual Interests." *Academe,* 1992, 78(6), 22–26.

Thompson, M. D. "Informal Student-Faculty Interaction: Its Relationship to Educational Gains in Science and Mathematics Among Community College Students." *Community College Review,* 2001, 29(1), pp. 35–55.

Tinto, V. *Leaving College: Rethinking the Causes and Cures of Student Attrition.* Chicago: University of Chicago Press, 1993.

U.S. Department of Education. *Instructional Faculty and Staff in Public 2-Year Colleges* (NCES 2000–192). Washington, D.C.: U.S. Department of Education, 2000.

U.S. Department of Education. *Background Characteristics, Work Activities and Compensation of Faculty and Instructional Staff in Postsecondary Institutions: Fall 1998.* National Study of Postsecondary Faculty, 1999 (NCES 2001–152). Washington, D.C.: U.S. Department of Education, 2001.

PAM SCHUETZ is a doctoral student in the Graduate School of Education and Information Studies at the University of California–Los Angeles and a former student trustee at Santa Monica College, California.

5

This chapter discusses differing attitudes of faculty toward students, using results from three national studies that compare community college faculty with faculty at four-year institutions and from a recent study conducted by the Center for the Study of Community Colleges to examine differences within subgroups of two-year faculty.

Faculty Attitudes About Students

Carol A. Kozeracki

Since the inception of the community college at the turn of the last century, the high priority assigned to the teaching role of the faculty has been unquestioned (Cohen and Brawer, 1996; Vaughan, 2000). From the perspective of the instructor, this means that the time and effort spent in the service of student learning are greater for community college faculty than for faculty at institutions with research requirements, which includes virtually all four-year colleges and universities. "They care for students, not research; for information transmission, not knowledge generation" (Cohen and Brawer, 1977, p. 46). Clearly, the mission of the community college calls for the faculty to create a classroom environment that is conducive to learning, but does it encourage something more? Are the attitudes of community college faculty toward students different from those of four-year faculty? And among community college faculty, do attitudes differ by teaching status or educational experience? This chapter will explore these questions using results from recent national studies.

The first section of this chapter will look at some of the differences in attitudes about students between community college faculty and faculty at four-year institutions, using findings from three national studies:

1. The Higher Education Research Institute's (HERI) faculty survey, "The American College Teacher," of 33,785 full-time faculty members who teach undergraduates, including 2,308 from community colleges.
2. The National Opinion Research Center's (NORC) "The American Faculty Poll" of 1,511 full-time faculty who teach undergraduate courses, including 507 two-year college faculty.

3. The Carnegie Foundation for the Advancement of Teaching's 1997 "National Survey of Faculty," which includes 5,151 full-time and part-time faculty

The following topics will be explored: faculty commitment to teaching and students, attitudes about student preparation, the perceived role of the faculty and the college, and how these factors affect satisfaction levels.

The second section will examine the different attitudes of two sub-groups of community college faculty toward students, using the findings from the Center for the Study of Community Colleges' (CSCC's) 2000 faculty survey. The subgroups are (1) part-timers and full-timers and (2) faculty with doctorates and those without.

External Comparisons

How do community college faculty view their students and the obligations they and their institutions have to their students? How do these views compare with those of faculty at four-year institutions? This section explores results from three national surveys that address the following topics: commitment to students and teaching, student preparation, the role of the college, and the effect of these issues on faculty satisfaction.

Commitment to Students and Teaching. Because of their institutions' commitment to teaching, community college instructors spend more time with students than faculty in other sectors of higher education and are more focused on teaching as their central responsibility. Responses to the 1998–1999 HERI faculty survey indicate that 97 percent of full-time community college faculty and 89 percent of four-year college and university faculty feel that teaching is their principal activity (Sax, Astin, Korn, and Gilmartin, 1999). The 1999 National Study of Postsecondary Faculty (NCES, 2001) finds that full-time community college faculty teach an average of 17.2 hours per week compared with 11.0 hours for faculty in all higher education institutions. Despite the differences in teaching load, community college faculty are about as likely as four-year college faculty to indicate that their teaching load is satisfactory or very satisfactory and are less likely to state that the teaching load is a source of stress (Sax, Astin, Korn, and Gilmartin, 1999).

The HERI survey also finds that 78 percent of community college faculty and 68 percent of four-year faculty feel that "opportunities for teaching" are a very important reason for pursuing an academic career. The NORC American Faculty Poll finds that more community college instructors than four-year faculty (93 percent vs. 84 percent) believe that the opportunity to educate students is "very important" to them personally (Sanderson, Phua, and Herda, 2000). The Carnegie study finds a gap between the percentage of community college faculty who state that undergraduate teaching is very important to them personally (82 percent) and the overall faculty respondents (71 percent) who express this sentiment (Huber, 1998). These findings illustrate that the primary interests of community college faculty appear to reflect the mission of these institutions.

Student Preparation and Performance. Most community colleges are open-admissions institutions, in keeping with their commitment to maximizing access. Therefore, it is not surprising that the community college faculty are more likely than their four-year colleagues to describe their students as being underprepared for college-level work. The HERI survey finds that only 20 percent of community college faculty and 31 percent of four-year faculty agree that most students are well prepared academically (Sax, Astin, Korn, and Gilmartin, 1999). The Carnegie Foundation study (Huber, 1998) shows that more than two-thirds of community college faculty disagree that their students are well prepared in mathematics, quantitative reasoning, and oral and written communication. These figures are substantially higher than for faculty at four-year institutions.

The HERI survey respondents indicate that 32 percent of community college faculty and 45 percent of four-year faculty are satisfied or very satisfied with the quality of the students. Sanderson, Phua, and Herda (2000) find that only 10 percent of community college faculty are "very satisfied" with the quality of the students, compared with faculty from four-year public (14 percent) and four-year private institutions (19 percent).

Despite these rather pessimistic assessments of student preparation and performance, the vast majority of community college faculty (87 percent) agree that "access to higher education should be available to all who meet minimum entrance requirements" (Huber, 1998). This seems to indicate that community college faculty are committed to the policy of providing education to all who might benefit, a central tenet of most community colleges' mission statement. However, the wording of the statement raises a question of interpretation in the context of an open-admissions institution. Are the faculty agreeing that "education should be available to all," or that there should be "minimum entrance requirements" to meet? This is especially provocative in light of the finding from the same survey that 71 percent of community college faculty agree that their institutions spend too much time and money teaching students what they should have learned in high school. Is there a disconnect between the students that faculty would like to teach and the students that the colleges are committed to serving?

Given the faculty's relatively negative perception of the academic qualifications of community college students overall, it would seem likely that they would not be satisfied with their own students. However, they are more likely than faculty at all other institutions, with the exception of liberal arts colleges, to agree that "overall, I'm pleased with my undergraduates" (Huber, 1998). Furthermore, an enthusiastic 95 percent of community college faculty are very or somewhat satisfied with their relationships with students (Huber, 1998). Clearly, there is some element of the relationship between faculty and students that the surveys are not capturing. Faculty

Table 5.1. Percent Rating Goals Noted as "Essential" or "Very Important" for Undergraduates

Goal	Two-Year Faculty	Four-Year Faculty
Develop moral character	64%	56%
Provide for emotional development	48%	35%
Help develop personal values	66%	58%
Enhance self-understanding	67%	60%
Prepare for responsible citizenship	64%	59%

Source: The American College Teacher: National Norms for the 1998–99 HERI Faculty Survey

express dissatisfaction with students' academic preparation and performance but are very satisfied with their relationships with students. Perhaps there are other aspects of student development, such as social or emotional growth, with which faculty are concerned. It is possible that student growth in these areas is responsible for high overall levels of faculty satisfaction with their students. The next section examines these issues.

The Role of the College. What should a student be able to expect from a college education in terms of both personal development and educational outcomes? A number of the surveys asked faculty about the level of faculty concern for students, the role of the college in developing students' personal skills, and the outcomes students should achieve as a result of their college experience.

In terms of concern expressed for the well-being of the students, the HERI survey found that 86 percent of community college faculty, compared with 73 percent of four-year faculty, agreed that faculty are interested in students' personal problems (Sax, Astin, Korn, and Gilmartin, 1999). In addition, more community college faculty agree that "faculty here are strongly interested in the academic problems of undergraduate students," compared with four-year faculty (88 percent vs. 80 percent). Huber (1998) found virtually identical results, and also found that more than half of all faculty agreed that faculty should spend more time with students outside the classroom

The faculty were also asked about the role of the college in helping students to develop personal qualities, such as self-knowledge and moral values. As shown in Table 5.1, the HERI survey (Sax, Astin, Korn, and Gilmartin, 1999) reveals some interesting differences in faculty perceptions about the importance of certain educational goals for undergraduates.

The community college faculty clearly feel that their institutions should be playing a significant role in helping students to shape their values and moral characters. However, they do not necessarily believe that their colleges have set these items as a priority. When faculty were asked about the priority given to personal development issues at their institutions, the differences between the four- and two-year college faculty virtually disappeared. No significant differences are found in the institutional priority assigned to helping students understand values, teaching students how to change society, and developing leadership ability in students (Sax, Astin, Korn, and Gilmartin, 1999). The Carnegie study (Huber, 1998) finds similar disparities between the priority that faculty and institutions place on student development in the areas of self-knowledge and firm moral values. Based on the results from these two surveys, it appears that the community college faculty, even more than the four-year college faculty, are interested in having their colleges play a stronger role in shaping the personal development of their students.

Finally, each of the surveys asked the faculty how well their institutions were providing students with appropriate academic outcomes, namely increased knowledge and career training. The Carnegie study finds that the community college faculty are positive about their colleges' responses to these obligations. One-third of the faculty feel their college does an excellent job in providing students with a general education. This percentage is substantially higher than responses for all sectors other than liberal arts colleges. Community college and liberal arts faculty are also most likely to rank their institutions as "excellent" in terms of providing undergraduates with the opportunity to explore personal interests through electives. Not surprisingly, given the emphasis of the community college on providing vocational training, community college faculty are more than twice as likely as faculty in any other sector to rank as excellent their colleges' ability to provide career preparation (Huber, 1998).

In response to a HERI survey question asking about the importance of employment preparation as a goal for undergraduates, 82 percent of two-year faculty and 67 percent of four-year faculty rank it as essential or very important (Sax, Astin, Korn, and Gilmartin, 1999). That survey also asked for an opinion on the following statement: "The chief benefit of a college education is that it increases one's earning power." Forty percent of community college faculty and 23 percent of four-year faculty agree. Despite the priority they assign to fostering the personal development of students, this strong level of agreement among community college faculty is a very powerful affirmation that a substantial number believe that the bottom line for students is, ultimately, job training.

Internal Comparisons

Since the 1960s, the decade of greatest growth in the community college professoriate, studies have shown that the community college faculty are not a monolithic group. Garrison (1967) finds so much internal diversity among community college instructors that traditional scales used to assess four-year faculty are not relevant. More recent studies underscore the fact that the faculty "are both increasingly diverse and increasingly fragmented from one another" (Outcalt, 2002, p. 259). Differences in attitudes by teaching status and educational experience have been uncovered by a number of researchers (Kelly, 1991; Rifkin, 1998). Therefore, it is worthwhile to explore the differing attitudes of subgroups within the community college professoriate.

In fall of 2000, the Center for the Study of Community Colleges (CSCC) surveyed 1,531 randomly selected faculty (77 percent response rate) from 109 community colleges across the country, using an updated version of a survey administered by CSCC in 1975 (Cohen and Brawer, 1977). (For more details on the method used in this study, see the "Editor's Introduction.") For this chapter, two subgroups of faculty were selected to be compared on a series of questions related to concern for students: part-timers and full-timers, and faculty with doctorates and those without. An analysis of variance was run on responses to nineteen questions for these two subgroups. The questions address the following issues:

- Faculty perception of the quality of their relation with students and of the value of students as a source of teaching advice
- Whether the instructor received a teaching award or developed extracurricular activities for students
- Time spent with students and with reading students' papers outside class
- The appropriate role of students in faculty evaluation
- Trends in student and institutional quality
- A ranking of the most important outcomes for an undergraduate education (from a choice of career knowledge, mastery of a discipline, preparation for transfer, self-knowledge, and interest in community)—items included because they reflect the faculty's perception of what a college owes to its students

The statistically significant differences (at the .01 level, except when specified) are presented below.

Part-Time and Full-Time Faculty. The largest number of significant differences is found between part-time and full-time faculty. (See Chapters Four and Six in this volume for further analysis of differences in faculty practices and attitudes on the basis of employment status.) Part-time faculty, who make up 35 percent of the respondents, are more likely to describe their students' enthusiasm for learning as excellent and to agree that faculty promotions should be based on formal student evaluations of their teachers. (For this chapter, faculty are categorized as part-time if they did not indicate full-time employment at any college.) The response to the latter question is largely hypothetical, as part-time faculty tend to be outside the promotion system. Part-time faculty are more likely to describe their relationships with their students as excellent and to rate their students as quite useful sources of advice on teaching (both significant at the .05 level). The first finding is unexpected given the fact that most part-time faculty are not paid for office hours and, according to the CSCC survey, spend less time with their students outside class. According to these results, it appears that part-time faculty find their academic interactions with students to be more positive than do the full-time faculty.

The full-time faculty are more likely to have received an award for teaching and to have developed extracurricular activities for their students. They also spent about 50 percent more time with students outside class during their last work day than did part-time faculty, and are more likely to wish they spent less time grading students' papers outside class. These results make sense given the higher number of courses taught and the greater amount of time spent on campus each day. Full-time faculty are more likely to agree that students are not as well prepared as they were five years ago, and they disagree more strongly than part-time faculty (significant at the .05 level) that students at their colleges are not receiving as good an education as they were five years ago. These two findings seem to indicate that full-time faculty believe their colleges are continuing to provide a high-quality education for an increasingly challenging student population.

In terms of ranking the qualities that students should gain from a two-year college education, the only difference that appears is that part-time faculty, somewhat surprisingly, are more likely to cite "preparation for further formal education" as a more important outcome than are the full-time faculty.

Earned Doctorates. Significant differences were identified between the responses of faculty with (16 percent of total respondents) and without doctoral degrees. Not surprisingly, having an advanced degree affects the instructors' perceptions about the important goals for a community college education. Those with doctorates are most likely to rank "preparation for further formal education" as the most important goal, followed by "knowledge and skills directly applicable to their careers." Instructors without doctorates indicate the reverse order of importance. This finding also makes sense given the greater likelihood that an instructor with a doctorate is teaching in a liberal arts field rather than in a technical or career field.

On all three questions relating to adult students and community education, faculty with doctorates are more outspoken in asking for greater college support. They feel more strongly than other faculty that their college should offer more cultural activities for adults in the community and are less likely to agree that their college provides enough courses and sufficient counseling and guidance for adult students. Again, this might be related to their own experiences with continued education and the value they place on access.

Finally, instructors with doctorates indicate that they find their students' enthusiasm for learning to be a little lower than their colleagues do. This may be the result of their own experiences in graduate school, where they were interacting with students whose academic achievement and interest in learning were extremely high, especially compared with lower-division students. One related, but unexpected, finding is that faculty who have doctorates are slightly more likely to have received an award for teaching (significant at the .05 level). One of the perennial concerns expressed about hiring faculty with doctorates for community college teaching is that they are socialized toward research rather than teaching. This finding indicates that these instructors find a way to make their training relevant to the classroom.

Summary and Recommendations

This chapter was designed to examine two questions: (1) Are the attitudes of community college faculty toward students different from those of faculty at four-year institutions? And (2) among community college faculty, do attitudes differ by teaching status or educational background?

The responses to the first question are almost paradoxical. Community college faculty very strongly assert that they are committed to teaching and that educating students is very important to them personally. Yet on a variety of measures, they express dissatisfaction with the academic preparation and quality of their students. In spite of these findings, the vast majority of faculty are satisfied with their relationships with their students, and they are more likely than other faculty to be pleased "overall" with their undergraduates. What is responsible for these results? Although no direct questions are asked in any of the surveys to respond to this issue, the subject is covered tangentially in questions about the goals of an undergraduate education. Through these responses, faculty indicate that the development of affective and social skills, including moral values and self-understanding, are important goals. Perhaps the role they are able to play in contributing to students' personal growth leads to increased feelings of satisfaction. Their responses also indicate that the colleges do not place a high priority on these goals. It would be useful for future faculty surveys to ask a wider range of questions about the relationship between faculty satisfaction and students.

In looking at the internal differences among subgroups of faculty, it is apparent that variety exists in faculty attitudes about students. Although this analysis does not conclude that one group or another is a better fit at a community college, the specific examples presented may be helpful to a college when making personnel decisions. For example, a college that is interested in emphasizing transfer may want to look more closely at faculty candidates with doctorates because of their belief that preparing students for further formal education is a college's most important responsibility to its students.

References

Cohen, A. M., and Brawer, F. B. *The Two-Year College Instructor Today.* New York: Praeger Special Studies, 1977.

Cohen, A. M., and Brawer, F. B. *The American Community College* (3rd ed.). San Francisco: Jossey-Bass, 1996.

Garrison, R. H. *Junior College Faculty: Issues and Problems; A Preliminary National Appraisal.* Washington, D.C.: American Association of Community and Junior Colleges, 1967.

Huber, M. T. *Community College Faculty Attitudes and Trends, 1997.* Menlo Park, Calif.: The Carnegie Foundation for the Advancement of Teaching, 1998.

Kelly, D. *Part-Time Faculty in the Community College: A Study of Their Qualifications, Frustrations, and Involvement.* Paper presented at the annual forum of the Association for Institutional Research, San Francisco, 1991.

National Center for Education Statistics. *Background Characteristics, Work Activities, and Compensation of Faculty and Instructional Staff in Postsecondary Institutions: Fall 1998* (NCES 2001–152). Washington, D.C.: U.S. Department of Education, 2001.

Outcalt, C. L. "A Profile of the Community College Professoriate, 1975–2000." Unpublished doctoral dissertation, University of California–Los Angeles, 2002.

Rifkin, T. "Differences Between the Professional Attitudes of Full- and Part-Time Community College Faculty." Paper presented at the American Association of Community Colleges Convention, Miami, April 1998

Sanderson, A., Phua, V. C., and Herda, D. *The American Faculty Poll.* Chicago: National Opinion Research Center, 2000.

Sax, L. J., Astin, A. W., Korn, W. S., and Gilmartin, S. K. *The American College Teacher: National Norms for the 1998–1999 HERI Faculty Survey.* Los Angeles: Higher Education Research Institute, University of California–Los Angeles, 1999.

Vaughan, G. B. *The Community College Story* (2nd ed.). Washington, D.C.: Community College Press, 2000.

CAROL A. KOZERACKI is the assistant director for the ERIC Clearinghouse for Community Colleges and a project manager in the office of institutional research at Santa Monica College, California.

PART THREE

Challenges and Opportunities for Community College Faculty

6

This chapter focuses on similarities and differences between part- and full-time faculty demographics, work profiles, attitudes and motives, and opinions about teaching and learning.

Part-Time Faculty: Competent and Committed

David W. Leslie and Judith M. Gappa

Community college faculty, by head count, are predominantly part-time. Only 35 percent of faculty at public two-year colleges were full-time in 1995, according to data from the National Center for Education Statistics [http://nces.ed.gov/pubs2000/Digest99/]. Although this trend has been evident for at least two decades (Gappa and Leslie, 1993; Cohen and Brawer, 1996), few detailed descriptions of part-time faculty in two-year colleges are available to establish who they are, what they do, and how they differ from their full-time colleagues.

The popular image of part-time faculty, as presented in frequent stories and opinion pieces in the media, perpetuates the commonly held assumption that part-timers are a temporary and dissatisfied lot who patch together part-time jobs by teaching at several institutions simultaneously and queue up for academic career opportunities that seem more and more scarce all the time. This picture is partly accurate for some part-time faculty, but it is substantially inaccurate for a very large portion of them. Instead, part-time faculty are usually employed elsewhere in full-time professional positions, have taught for at least several years at their employing

---

The analyses underlying this chapter were compiled before release of NSOPF-99. However, review of the NSOPF-99 data suggests little change exists in the overall character and composition of the part-time teaching workforce in community colleges. Changes do appear in the motivations of individuals and the incentives they respond to when entering part-time teaching jobs. But the 1993 and 1999 data lack sufficient comparability on key items that would allow a valid comparison. External conditions for part-timers may have changed, but the people and how institutions employ them seem to have remained largely the same.

institutions, do not seek full-time academic work, and are more motivated by the intrinsic satisfactions they find in teaching than by economic or career interests (Gappa and Leslie, 1997).

For all the published work advocating better treatment of part-timers, and for all the debates over whether institutions damage themselves and the integrity of academic work by relying on them, there remains a serious gap in our understanding of part-timers' teaching in community colleges. This chapter summarizes findings from analyses of two databases, a survey of community college faculty conducted by the Center for the Study of Community Colleges (CSCC), and the National Survey of Postsecondary Faculty conducted in 1992–93 by the National Center for Education Statistics.

Methods

Data for this chapter came from a national survey of 2,000 community college faculty members at 114 institutions conducted by the CSCC. (See "Editor's Notes" for more details on the CSCC study.) We also relied on corroborating data from the restricted-use file of responses to the National Survey of Postsecondary Faculty conducted in 1992–1993 by the National Center for Education Statistics (NSOPF-93). Responses were received from 25,780 full- and part-time faculty members in a random sample of 31,354 to whom survey instruments were sent. Technical information about the sample, response rate, measurement and sampling error, and weighting of the data is reported in Kirshstein, Matheson, Jing, and Zimbler (1997). We used cross-tabulations, chi-square statistics, and t-tests for independent samples to derive descriptions of part-time faculty in community colleges.

Results

The CSCC survey provides new data for comparison with the data collected in NSOPF surveys. The picture of part-time faculty in community colleges portrayed by both surveys is consistent with and enhances the overall picture of community college faculty drawn from prior studies. We present and compare the data from both surveys in four parts: demographics, work profile, attitudes and motives, and opinions about teaching and learning.

Demographics. Who are the part-time faculty in community colleges? Both surveys show that like their full-time colleagues, part-timers are equally likely to be men or women. Part-timers are slightly more likely to be *both* older and younger than full-time faculty, although the mean age of part-timers is 45.8 years while the mean age for full-timers is 48 years. Variance of age is greater among part-timers, with over twice as many (proportionately) in the over 65 bracket and nearly twice as many in the 25–34 bracket as full-time faculty.

Part-time faculty typically *average* five to six years of teaching experience, compared with eleven to twelve years for full-time faculty. Both databases are consistent on these estimates. But perhaps more important, over half of all part-time faculty members in community colleges have five or more years of experience at their current institutions, according to the CSCC data. Very nearly one-third (30 percent) report over ten years of teaching at their current institutions. This is consistent with data from NSOPF-93, which also shows a higher level of employment stability at single institutions than is commonly assumed for part-time faculty, although at lower rates than those reported by the CSCC survey. These data indicate that part-timers are a stable component of the faculty workforce in community colleges, with considerable teaching experience on average.

NSOPF-93 data show that half of all part-timers (52 percent) hold master's degrees and 62 percent of full-time faculty in community colleges hold the same degree. Roughly 9 percent of both groups report working on a doctorate. Full-time faculty members are more likely to hold doctorates (18 percent vs. 11 percent of part-timers according to the CSCC survey, and just slightly fewer in both cases according to NSOPF). Eighty percent of both full- and part-time community college faculty report that they are not presently working on advanced degrees. These data suggest little incentive (or support) for community college faculty to pursue terminal academic degrees, which usually are not required in any event. On the whole, part-time faculty in community colleges have achieved a slightly lower level of education than full-time faculty, but probably not so much lower that it would raise clear concerns about differences in "quality." Part-time faculty are more likely to teach occupational or professional subjects for which the doctorate is either uncommon or not relevant (Leslie, 1998). No recent studies of part-time faculty have found any differences in the quality of instruction provided by full- and part-time faculty (Cohen and Brawer, 1996; Grubb, 1999; Gappa and Leslie, 1993; Wyles, 1998).

The CSCC survey asks about numbers of different kinds of journals read by the respondents. These data show no statistically significant differences ($p > .01$) between part- and full-time faculty with respect to disciplinary journals, general media (such as the *Chronicle of Higher Education*) dealing with higher education, and journals focusing specifically on community colleges. Full-time faculty are slightly more disposed to read discipline-based journals, while part-timers are slightly more disposed to read general media. If these patterns are reflective of some underlying pattern of intellectual curiosity or commitment to professional or disciplinary currency, the data suggest that "no difference" is the safest conclusion. In the NSOPF survey, part-time faculty do not report spending a substantially different amount of time on "professional development" (5.8 percent vs. 4.6 percent for full-timers), and they also report being more satisfied with their ability to keep up with developments in their fields (67.9 percent vs. 48.3 percent for full-time faculty)(Leslie, 1998).

Work Profile. According to the CSCC survey, half (51 percent) of all part-time faculty respondents are employed elsewhere in nonteaching jobs (vs. about 70 percent reported by Cohen and Brawer, 1996), and nearly two-thirds of them (61 percent) work more than thirty hours a week at those jobs. In the NSOPF-93 survey, nearly 80 percent (78.2 percent) of community college part-timers report holding other jobs. Two-thirds of these part-timers say the other jobs are full-time, and just short of 38 percent report that the other jobs involve teaching. Thus data from the two surveys confirm other reports (Gappa and Leslie, 1993; Gappa and Leslie, 1997) that part-timers are at least as likely to be employed elsewhere in business or professional occupations as in teaching part- or full-time, and that part-timers who have more than one postsecondary teaching job at a time appear to number between 15 and 17 percent of all part-time community college faculty. This is a far smaller figure than popular impressions might suggest, and is congruent with the taxonomy we propose in *The Invisible Faculty* (1993). We suggest there that most part-timers are "specialists, experts and professionals" with their primary occupations outside the academy, "free lancers" who prefer to work simultaneously at several different part-time occupations, or "career enders" in transition from well-established careers outside of higher education. We found relatively few part-timers who are "aspiring academics" fully qualified for and actively seeking full-time faculty careers (pp. 43–65).

Community college faculty, whether full- or part-time, spend their workdays in very similar activities. The CSCC survey shows that on a given workday, both put in between six and seven hours teaching, planning classes, and interacting with students. Full-time faculty spend significantly ($p<.01$) more time on administration, teaching, and interacting with students. (See Chapter Four for a detailed exploration of differences in instructional practice by employment status; see also Chapter Five for an analysis of differences in faculty attitudes toward students on the basis of employment status.)

There is little in these data to suggest that the popular image of part-time faculty as underqualified, nomadic, or inadequately attentive to their responsibilities has any validity. To the contrary, the portrait that emerges shows part-time faculty in community colleges to be stable professionals with substantial experience and commitment to their work. This is in keeping with the findings of Grubb in *Honored but Invisible* (1999), although he and his associates come to many of these conclusions via a different route.

Motives, Attitudes, and Morale. NSOPF data show that half (51 percent) of all part-timers in community colleges prefer to teach part-time. There is no difference in the preferences between men and women, but more women (52 percent) than men (42 percent) respond that they teach part-time because full-time opportunities are not available, indicating perhaps that women have less flexibility in moving to find those opportunities. Men (70 percent) are far more likely than women (52 percent) to be teaching part-time to supplement their incomes. About two-thirds of both groups report teaching part-time to "be in an academic environment." Almost none (8 percent) teach part-time while pursuing graduate degrees—with only negligible differences between men and women. Yet this group of part-time doctoral seekers, while a very small part of the sample, differs substantially and systematically from other respondents in the CSCC survey.

Part-time faculty members appear generally satisfied with their jobs. The CSCC data show no difference between part- and full-time faculty members' rating of the "working environment in general." They both rate it 1.9 on a scale where 1.0 means "excellent" and 2.0 means "good." The only aspects of their jobs that part-time faculty rate less than "good" are salary (2.7) and job security (2.6), where 3.0 means "fair". These patterns parallel responses to NSOPF's similar items. On the NSOPF survey, over 85 percent of part-timers respond that they are satisfied or very satisfied with their jobs on the whole compared with 84 percent of full-timers (Leslie 1998).

Statistically, part-time faculty rate their own autonomy, relations with administrators, and students' enthusiasm for learning more favorably than do full-time faculty. In the CCSC survey, part-timers are slightly, but significantly ($p<.001$), more likely than full-time faculty to agree that their institutions' administration is "creative and effective," although both groups provide a mildly positive assessment. They also report being less stressed than full-time faculty ($p<.001$). Full-time faculty rate their own freedom to choose instructional materials more favorably than do part-time faculty.

In other respects, full- and part-time faculty in community colleges do not differ in rating various aspects of their jobs—and generally report those ratings to be in the "good" to "excellent" range. Both part- and full-time faculty would choose academic work again, given the choice. The data from both surveys corroborate these points by showing that part-time faculty are not as massively or universally dissatisfied with their jobs as is popularly assumed. To the contrary, they are generally very satisfied.

Faculty professionalism, and whether or not it is supported by the institution, is a recurrent theme in academic labor relations (Rhoades, 1998). The CSCC survey asks several questions bearing on unionization. Full-time faculty "somewhat agree" that collective bargaining "has a definite place in a community college." Part-timers differ, responding in the direction of "no opinion." The NSOPF data show that just over 50 percent of full-time community college faculty belong to unions, compared with only 17 percent of part-timers. This difference is to be expected when most part-timers have primary jobs elsewhere and fewer guarantees of job security as faculty members, and when only 39 percent of the collective bargaining contracts that address part-time faculty issues in some respect speak to their rights or perquisites (Rhoades, p. 157).

Full-time faculty are significantly ($p<.001$) less receptive to merit pay than are part-time faculty, but both are mildly supportive. But the pay issue on which part- and full-time faculty most emphatically part ways asks whether part-timers "should be paid the same, per class taught, as full-timers." Part-timers are statistically ($p<.001$) more likely to agree than full-timers, who are ambivalent about pay. On a politically potent pocket-book issue, this difference in attitude could lead to conflict between the two groups, particularly when budgets are tight. Full-timers who support collective bargaining also support equal pay. Younger full-time faculty—who are more supportive of collective bargaining and less supportive of merit pay—are more likely to support equal pay for equal work by part-timers.

Both full- (mean of 3.1) and part-time (mean of 3.0 where 3.0 means "no opinion") community college faculty show uncertainty about whether "claims of discriminatory practices against women and minority faculty and administrators have been greatly exaggerated." NSOPF data show a more positive assessment, as both part- and full-time community college faculty agree that women and minority faculty are treated fairly.

Opinions About Teaching and Learning. Part- and full-time faculty members are in substantial agreement about the overall functions of community colleges according to the CSCC survey results. They rate providing students with job-entry skills and prebaccalaureate transfer functions as essentially coequal priorities. Career-skill upgrading is ranked third, with lifelong learning, remedial education, and community development ranked in sequence as lower priorities.

Similarly there are almost no differences between part- and full-time faculty in the predominant instructional methods used. Lectures, student discussions, and exams account for close to two-thirds of all class time regardless of whether the instructor is part- or full-time. Lab work accounts for another substantial portion among full-time faculty (about 7 percent), but less for part-time faculty (4 percent), the one significant difference between the two groups.

On several other measures in the CSCC survey, however, part-time faculty members appear less committed, accomplished, and creative in their teaching than full-time faculty. For example, they are significantly ($p<.001$) less likely to have received an award for outstanding teaching (24 percent vs. 39 percent of full-timers), taught with someone from outside their department (15 percent vs. 24 percent), revised a course syllabus within the last three years (88 percent vs. 97 percent), prepared a multimedia presentation for class (42 percent vs. 53 percent), or attended a professional conference in the last three years (67 percent vs. 89 percent). However, to assume that these differences are indicative of overall quality of teaching performance would be erroneous without understanding why the differences occur. For example, part-timers may or may not be eligible for teaching awards or to receive financial assistance with expenses associated with attending professional conferences. They may be teaching courses that have multiple sections and standard syllabi, allowing less opportunity for course development. To the extent that they are marginalized in their departments, they may have no voice in curricular development or textbook selection (Wyles, 1998). It is difficult to interpret these differences, and additional research is needed.

Over three-fourths of both full-time (83 percent) and part-time (76 percent) faculty at community colleges indicate that they are motivated to pursue professional development. However they vary according to what type of professional development they want. Significantly ($p<.001$) more full-time faculty seek in-service opportunities, whereas more part-time faculty are interested in options to complete advanced degrees. Both full- and part-time faculty "somewhat agree" that faculty should "take some type of academic course work or engage in a creative activity at least every three years."

Neither full- nor part-time faculty appear to feel strongly that their institutions should provide more faculty development opportunities to support teaching directly. They "agree somewhat" that instructors in their fields "are well-prepared to teach." And, they show virtually identical "no opinion" scores on an item asserting that their institutions do "too little to orient new faculty." These findings run counter to the actual academic preparation and experience part-timers have vis à vis their full-time faculty colleagues, and one would assume greater differences on this issue between full- and part-timers. Although they "somewhat agree" that students "are not as well prepared" as previously, both part-time and full-time faculty *disagree* somewhat with the statement that students are not receiving as good an education as they did five years ago. The general picture from the CSCC survey appears to be that institutions are supportive of faculty who are dealing reasonably well with an incrementally less well-prepared student population.

Conclusion

The picture of part-time community college faculty that emerges from this analysis is—on the whole—consistent with those of previous studies. Part-timers in community colleges look more like full-time faculty than is sometimes assumed. Their interests, attitudes, and motives are relatively similar. They are experienced, stable professionals who find satisfaction in teaching. Contrary to popular images, only a small fraction of part-timers are eagerly seeking full-time positions and subsisting on starvation wages while holding multiple part-time jobs—the prevalent stereotype so often profiled in the popular media.

On the other hand, this analysis of the CSCC data does show that part-time community college faculty members appear to be more comfortable with conventional teaching practices and less likely to have won outstanding teaching awards. However, these data can also be interpreted to mean that while they do, on average, have substantial teaching experience, they are less seasoned than full-time faculty, and perhaps less secure about breaking the mold. Certainly this conclusion makes sense when the lack of recognition, rewards, and job security available to part-timers are taken into account.

Part-timers do feel that their institutions have been appropriately supportive. But the relative strength of these feelings leaves room for improvement. Academic administrators at community colleges may want to read the data in the CSCC survey in two ways: that on one hand, the part-timers are evidently satisfied on the whole and are clearly able to do the job they are asked to do, and on the other, that institutions may see in these data a less than ringing affirmation of their preparation and the conditions under which they work. Part-timers are less likely than full-timers to have achieved graduate degrees. Just a little over half of the part-timers, for example, hold master's degrees, a minimal qualification to teach in an academic program at an accredited institution of higher education. The need for a graduate degree appears to be a high priority for part-timers among other options for professional development. Given that part-timers are also somewhat less experienced teachers and perhaps more wedded to conventional instructional methods, it would appear that their professional development needs cover both substantive disciplinary preparation and preparation to teach.

As we suggest elsewhere (Gappa and Leslie, 1993, 1997), part-time faculty should be considered an integral asset among all of those who teach. Investing in their capabilities—instead of treating them like replaceable parts—should yield long-term returns in teaching effectiveness, morale, and institutional loyalty.

References

Cohen, A., and Brawer, F. *The American Community College* (3rd ed.). San Francisco: Jossey-Bass, 1996.

Gappa, J. M., and Leslie, D. W. *The Invisible Faculty: Improving the Status of Part-Timers in Higher Education.* San Francisco: Jossey-Bass, 1993.

Gappa, J. M., and Leslie, D. W. "Two Faculties or One? The Conundrum of Part-Timers in a Bifurcated Work Force." Inquiry #6, New Pathways Working Paper Series. Washington, D.C.: American Association for Higher Education, 1997.

Grubb, N. W. *Honored but Invisible: An Inside Look at Teaching in Community Colleges.* New York: Routledge, 1999.

Kirshtein, R. J., Matheson, N., Jing, Z., and Zimbler, L. J. *Instructional Faculty and Staff in Higher Education Institutions: Fall 1987 and Fall 1992* (NCES 97–470). Washington, D.C.: U.S. Department of Education, 1997.

Leslie, D. W. "Part-Time, Adjunct, and Temporary Faculty: The New Majority?" Report to the Alfred P. Sloan Foundation. The College of William and Mary, Williamsburg, Va., 1998.

National Center for Education Statistics. "Digest of Education Statistics." U.S. Department of Education, 2000. [http://nces.ed.gov/pubs2000/Digest99/chapter3 .html]

Rhoades, Gary. *Managed Professionals: Unionized Faculty and Restructuring Academic Labor.* Albany: State University of New York Press, 1998.

Wyles, B. A. "Adjunct Faculty in the Community College: Reality and Challenges." In D. Leslie (ed.), *The Growing Use of Part-Time Faculty: Understanding Causes and Effects.* New Directions for Higher Education, no. 104. San Francisco: Jossey-Bass, 1998.

DAVID W. LESLIE *is chancellor professor of education at the College of William and Mary, Williamsburg, Virginia.*

JUDITH M. GAPPA *is professor of educational administration at Purdue University, West Lafayette, Indiana.*

*Despite the literature pointing to a "chilly climate" for
female students and faculty, there has been little attention
to the perceived conditions for women as community
college faculty members. This chapter provides a
literature review as well as analyses of a national dataset
of responses of community college faculty to examine the
climate at the nation's two-year colleges.*

Exploring the Climate for Women as Community College Faculty

Linda Serra Hagedorn and Berta Vigil Laden

Two decades ago Hall and Sandler coined the phrase "chilly climate" to symbolically represent a pervasive and negative classroom climate reported by girls and women. Subsequently, the term has been applied to women's experiences in postsecondary classrooms and career advancement. Hall and Sandler's (1982) groundbreaking study notes that the traditional practices of college professors provide a differential treatment of students by gender that favors men and marginalizes women.

Other studies followed, focusing on women's perceptions of their career development, barriers, and opportunities in the academy. Discriminatory practices and attitudes toward women were documented, and evidence of restrictions on women's academic freedom and lower levels of advancement were shown to be more widespread than generally assumed. One of these studies also gave rise to the image of the "glass ceiling" as a composition of transparent barriers that prevented women from rising above a certain level in the institutional hierarchy (Morrison, White, Van Velsor, and The Center for Creative Leadership, 1987). A decade later the "academic funnel" provided a picture of decreasing opportunities for women as they struggled to progress to higher levels of administration.

Despite the prevalence of research literature with clear evidence of a chilly climate for many women college students, faculty, and administrators, little attention has been given to the status of women faculty at community colleges. Here we provide a literature review to highlight the conditions of women faculty working in colleges and universities and empirical analyses of a national dataset of community college faculty collected by the Center for the Study of Community Colleges (CSCC) to determine if similar conditions prevail for women faculty in two-year colleges. We ask: Is there a chilly climate at community colleges for women faculty?

Review of the Literature

According to Glazer-Raymo (1999), academic women face formidable challenges in combining marriage, motherhood, and career within a social climate of male dominance and assumed superiority. Glazer and Slater (1987) examine women's entry into academe from 1890 to 1940 and find that to counteract the myth of male superiority and innate suitability for academic life, women academics have to resort to "super performance" to be recognized as equals in their professional roles. Through analyses of a survey of women with doctorates, Astin (1969) demonstrates gender discrimination in tenure that directly leads to high attrition rates of women faculty. She also notes that many women academics juggle two lives, balancing families and the heavy demands of their professional careers.

Gilligan's (1977) controversial study on women's psychological development and ways of making choices and decisions boldly uncovers the blatantly obvious: previous studies had been limited to white, male, Western subjects. In addition, Gilligan defines and acknowledges the ethics of caring and being responsive to the needs of others. She contends that men and women differ in how they make decisions and judgments. She acknowledges that women employ a moral context of choice where the needs of individuals are not necessarily abstracted from general principles but can be determined inductively from the specific experiences each individual brings to a situation.

Expanding on Gilligan's work, Belenky, Clinchy, Goldberger, and Tarule (1986) analyze perspectives on knowing (i.e., silence, received knowing, subjective knowing, procedural knowing, and constructed knowing). Although these perspectives are not necessarily perceived as distinctively female, Belenky, Clinchy, Goldberger, and Tarule advance the concept that women's ways of knowing and thinking have been masked or distorted historically by ignoring women in psychological studies, and thus these studies present a masculine view as representative of the general population. They present an alternate image of women as focused on such characteristics as connectedness, cooperation, and working with others in "webs and nets" rather than in the pyramids and hierarchical ladders that are more typically male models of ascension.

Gilligan's and Belenky and his colleagues' findings lay the theoretical foundation for studies that follow examining women's and men's leadership styles. The concept that there are different styles of leadership possible—and not just the rational, linear model favored by men—also tacitly acknowledges that a chilly climate exists for women in professional surroundings.

The Conditions of Women Faculty

In considering women faculty's roles in higher education, it is clear that on average they spend more time teaching (58 percent vs. 46 percent) and much less time in research than men (16 percent vs. 27 percent) (Glazer-Raymo, 1999). However, it is difficult to ascertain if the differences are really due to personal preferences or to the types of postsecondary institutions at which more women work. It is important to point out that a research/teaching gap is likely a moot point in community colleges where teaching is the primary emphasis for all faculty and research and scholarship as exemplified in four-year institutions is not.

Additionally, we find that women remain concentrated in the disciplinary areas of the humanities, social sciences, and education and are uncommon in law, medicine, mathematics, physics, biology, and other hard sciences (Hagedorn, Nora, and Pascarella, 1996). Women faculty in the hard sciences report professional climates to be especially chilly. For these women, it is particularly difficult to achieve professional recognition in their male-dominated fields due to little to no mentoring for crucial career advancement, such as how to secure grants, set up research labs, hire research assistants, and garner other important institutional support (Glazer-Raymo, 1999; Wilson, 1999). Vetter (1992) states that a "triple penalty of cultural, attitudinal, and structural impediments" (p. 4) makes it much more difficult for women scientists to persevere in their professions.

Some women faculty manage to rise to positions of administrative leadership, such as program coordinator and department chair; perhaps they are seen as opportunities to move up the administrative career ladder into positions such as dean, vice president, and president. In many instances, assumptions about gender and power surface when women indicate interest in or make such career moves. Townsend (1995) states that those with structural power—typically men because they dominate positions of power—often respond by creating or maintaining structural barriers to block women's movement into positions of power and authority and thus exacerbate the already chilly climate by marginalizing women even more. Glazer-Raymo (1999) echoes the assertion: "The politics of leadership takes on a different meaning when gender becomes part of the equation" (p. 24).

Townsend (1995) contends that women fare better in community colleges than in four-year institutions due primarily to their larger representation and the presence of more women role models serving in positions of leadership. Frye (1995) states that several characteristics in the historical evolution of the two-year college create a more favorable environment for women. Frye surmises that community colleges' multiple missions lead to climates where students can exert significant influence on program decisions that may have positive repercussions for women students. He adds that the move to coeducation is easier because women students were welcomed earlier into these institutions, while the early practice of recruiting instructors from local high schools contributes to more women faculty.

Faculty Women of Color

A discussion of conditions for women faculty must acknowledge that women of color may experience even chillier climates than white women. Ignoring women's differences related to culture and race/ethnicity would be a glaring omission akin to that of Erikson's (1968) and others' psychological development studies of white men that assume that they represent the entire population. While Bower's study (Chapter Eight) focuses on faculty of color, we would be remiss if we did not specifically address *women* faculty of color's unique situations. Until the 1980s the limited research on women of color classified all women as an aggregate group, rather than focusing on a culturally specific race/ethnicity. Researchers such as Weis (1992), Rendón (1982, 1992), Turner (1988), Amey (1999), Amey and Twombly (1992), Twombly (1995), Laden (1994, 1999), Laden and Turner (1995), Townsend (1995), and Laden and Hagedorn (2000) include issues of race, class, and gender for diverse groups of students, faculty, and administrators in the community college.

The State of Women Faculty at Community Colleges

In this section we turn from the literature to a targeted look at the community college climate for women faculty in the new century. We first provide general statistics concerning gender and two-year colleges from the National Center for Education Statistics and the U.S. Department of Education. Second, we analyze a national dataset of the responses of over 1,500 community college faculty to test for indicators of a chilly climate as well as to elucidate the nature of the situation reported by women faculty.

A National Picture of Community Colleges. Over 5.6 million people are enrolled at one of the nation's 1,727 community college campuses that include over 57 percent women students (Digest of Education Statistics [Digest], 2000). Community colleges especially appeal to women students because they offer a number of programs and opportunities, including convenient class schedules, early childhood programs with extended child care, welfare reform programs, reentry and single-parent programs, women's centers, low tuition, and neighborhood locations.

Women's representation is also significantly larger among the approximately 301,000 faculty at community colleges, comprising 48.7 percent of the faculty vs. 36.3 percent at four-year institutions. However, both community colleges and four-year institutions have equally low representation of faculty of color. While the 2000 U.S. Census reports that 24.9 percent of

Table 7.1. Proportion of Female Faculty by Institutional Type (Percent)

	1974–75		1997–98	
Rank	Two-year college	All Institutions	Two-year college	All Institutions
Full Professor	28.2	10.1	37.6	18.7
Associate Professor	32.4	17.3	47.8	34.6
Assistant Professor	42.0	27.9	52.8	46.8
Instructor	50.0	48.0	53.7	58.6
Lecturer	2.5	41.4	55.6	55.6

Adapted from the AAUP Salary Surveys for 1974–75 and 1997–98.

the population is nonwhite (U.S. Department of Commerce, 2001), the proportion of faculty of color is 18.4 percent at public four-year colleges and 17.4 percent at community colleges (Digest, 2000). Regarding rank, we compare the 1974–1975 and 1997–1998 academic years (Table 7.1). In the four-year sector, women are located primarily in the lecturer and assistant professor ranks, fewer obtain tenure and promotion to associate professor, and even fewer become full professor (Astin, Antonio, Cress, and Astin, 1997). Although women are clearly better represented in the higher ranks at two-year colleges, there are still signs of inequality. While 74.8 percent of the men faculty are tenured, only 68.1 percent of the women faculty in community colleges enjoy the same status (Digest, 2000).

Taken together, the statistics appear to paint a somewhat more favorable climate for women faculty in community colleges than at four-year universities, but it is important to note that salary differentials still exist. In 1998–1999, the average salary for full-time community college male faculty was $48,961 compared with $45,457 for their female counterparts (AAUP, 2001). Using National Survey of Postsecondary Faculty dataset, Hagedorn (2000) finds that 73 percent of women faculty at four-year institutions are paid less than their male counterparts, with an average gender-based difference of $8,681. Such differences should not be taken lightly as Hagedorn (1996) finds in an earlier study using a separate national dataset that gender-based wage differentials for faculty contribute to women's departure from academia.

One reason salaries of community college faculty are less gender dependent may be the effect of collective bargaining (Castro, 2000). Women have successfully assumed leadership roles in faculty unions (Townsend, 1995), and the presence of those women may heighten awareness of salary equity within unionized campuses.

Examining the Community College Climate Using the Faculty Dataset. To test for a chilly climate among female faculty members, we designed analyses of the community college faculty dataset consisting of the responses of 743 male and 740 female faculty. We began by statistically testing for gender differences by ethnicity and age to see if women were over- or underrepresented among older faculty or faculty of color. Although we found that men were significantly older than women in the sample, differences in salary were still apparent within each age group. Note that while there are a larger proportion of men in the fifty-five to sixty-four age group, there are more women in all other age brackets. This age distribution is consistent with the national distribution by gender and age of faculty in public two-year colleges (National Center for Education Statistics, 2001). These data indicate trends in hiring younger faculty and more women faculty. Thus as older faculty retire, the distribution of men and women faculty may no longer exhibit such differentials.

We also compared the number of years as a faculty member and the number of years worked at the present college. We found that men reported significantly more experience as faculty members and reported working at their current college for a longer period of time.

We next measured the climate as reported by faculty. Using the literature as a guide, we examined (1) overall assessment of the climate, (2) satisfaction with salary, (3) satisfaction with students, (4) propensity to leave the college, (5) desire for more interaction with colleagues, and (6) attitudes toward discrimination. To test if men and women perceive their climate differently, we designed a multivariate analysis of covariance (MANCOVA) to test for differences by gender and ethnicity. Although our hypotheses centered on gender differences, we included ethnicity as a dependent variable because we wanted to test for interactive effects (i.e., is the climate more uncomfortable for women faculty of color than for white women faculty?). We used the MANCOVA because we wanted to control for differences in age and level of faculty experience that we earlier found to be significantly different by gender.[1] Our statistical analyses tested the null hypothesis that perceptions of climate do not differ by gender or ethnicity. The MANCOVA statistical method was appropriate with these data because the sample sizes of men and women were approximately equal and there were no signs of nonnormality within the variables that we intended to use. We first checked the correlations between the dependent variable (gender) and the covariates (age, time as a faculty member, and years worked at the college). We found a very high correlation between time as a faculty member, time at the current college, and age. We determined that age would serve as the single covariate in the final analysis. The final equation had two dependent variables (gender and ethnicity), five dependent variables (overall assessment of climate, satisfaction with salary, satisfaction with students, propensity to leave, and attitudes toward discrimination), and one covariate (age).

The multivariate test of the main effects indicate that there are significant differences by age, gender, and minority/nonminority status without a significant interaction between gender and ethnicity. The significant main effects indicate a need to examine the univariate results. However, we immediately noted that the eta in all cases was negligible, indicating that statistical significance should be weighed against practical considerations.

The tests of between-subjects effects (univariate analysis) reveal that the only independent variable with significant differences by gender or ethnicity is attitudes toward discrimination. Women and faculty of color are statistically more likely to disagree that claims of discriminatory practices against women and minorities have been greatly exaggerated than are men or white faculty.[2]

Conclusions

Using this national dataset of community college faculty, we find only a slight gender effect on measures pertaining to the perception of a chilly climate. It may be that the mission of equality has pervaded the faculty climate and has positively affected it. It appears that women faculty do not report higher levels of dissatisfaction or a greater propensity to leave academe. Further, it appears that for this sample of community college faculty, women perceive the climate similar to the way their male counterparts do. However, we do find statistical evidence of difference in perceptions of discrimination reported significantly higher by women than by men and even statistically higher by women faculty of color. Thus we do find some evidence that women of color perceive a different (chillier?) climate than white women. However, our findings on faculty of color must be weighed against the smaller number of faculty of color (11 percent of the sample) as compared with the entire sample. We caution, however, that although the majority of our news is positive, the finding on discrimination should not be taken too lightly, as it may indicate undercurrents of attitudes or events that we could not capture or measure in the items included in the questionnaire. We call for additional research to add a qualitative component to our analyses to better understand the climate for women faculty, especially women of color, and to provide a thick description of the working conditions perceived by all women faculty.

Further, it is imperative to stipulate that we performed a secondary data analyses on an existing dataset and hence our analyses suffers from a common malady of virtually all secondary studies. Specifically, we investigated a question that the designers of the questionnaire may not have previously considered. Also, the questionnaire does not include items measuring advancement to administration or involvement in decision making, both important constructs for measuring a chilly climate. Future research is needed to include the measures of climate that could not be included in our analyses.

We return to our original question: Is there a chilly climate at community colleges for women faculty? Certainly no analyses can categorically negate or affirm the climate at all campuses, but our assessment of a national dataset does provide some evidence that the climate at the average community college may be warmer than at four-year institutions. On the other hand, our analyses in no way indicate that community colleges are havens where women faculty are free from the confines of glass ceilings, academic funnels, or discrimination. We conclude with the knowledge that we continue to live in a gendered world (Wood, 1997), but that the gender politics may be a shade softer at community colleges where equality is embedded in the institutional mission.

Notes

1. MANCOVA increases the sensitivity of the test of main effects and interactions by reducing the error term as well as adjusts the means of the dependent variables to a level consistent with values if the subjects have been similar on the covariates (Tabachnick and Fidell, 1996)
2. The full analyses including reliability of the scales is available by contacting the first author.

References

American Association of University Professors. "The Annual Report on the Economic Status of the Profession 2000–2001," 2001. [http://www.aaup.org/z01tab.htm]

Amey, M. J. "Navigating the Raging River: Reconciling Issues of Identity, Inclusion, and Administrative Practice." In K. M. Shaw, J. R. Valadez, and R. A. Rhoads (eds.), *Community Colleges as Cultural Texts.* New York: State University of New York Press, 1999, pp. 59–82.

Amey, M. J., and Twombly, S. B. "Re-Visioning Leadership in Community Colleges." *The Review of Higher Education,* 1992, 15, 25–150.

Astin, H. S. *The Woman Doctorate in America: Origins, Career, and Family.* New York: Russell Sage, 1969.

Astin, H. S., Antonio, A. I., Cress, C. M., and Astin, A. W. *Race and Ethnicity in the American Professoriate, 1995–96.* Los Angeles: Higher Education Research Institute, University of California, 1997.

Belenky, M. F., Clinchy, B. J., Goldberger, N. R., and Tarule, J. M. *Women's Ways of Knowing: The Development of Self, Voice, and Mind.* New York: Basic Books, 1986.

Castro, C. R. "Community College Faculty Satisfaction and the Faculty Union." In L. S. Hagedorn (ed.), *What Contributes to Job Satisfaction Among Faculty and Staff.* New Directions For Institutional Research, no. 105. San Francisco: Jossey-Bass, 2000.

Erikson, E. *Identity: Youth and Crisis.* New York: Norton, 1968.

Frye, J. H. "Women in the Two-Year College, 1900 to 1970." In B. K. Townsend (ed.), *Gender and Power in the Community College.* New Directions for Community Colleges, no. 89. San Francisco: Jossey-Bass, 1995.

Gilligan, C. "In a Different Voice: Women's Conceptions of Self and of Morality." *Harvard Educational Review,* 1977, 47, 481–517.

Glazer, P. M., and Slater, M. *Unequal Colleagues: The Entrance of Women into the Professions, 1890–1940.* New Brunswick, N.J.: Rutgers University Press, 1987.

Glazer-Raymo, J. *Shattering the Myths: Women in Academe.* Baltimore: The Johns Hopkins University Press, 1999.

Hagedorn, L. S. "Wage Equity and Women Faculty Job-Satisfaction: The Role of Wage Differentials in a Job Satisfaction Causal Model." *Research in Higher Education,* 1996, 37(5), 569–598.

Hagedorn, L. S. "Gender Differences in Faculty Productivity, Satisfaction, and Salary: What Really Separates Us?" Shaping a National Agenda for Women in Higher Education. Conference Proceedings, University of Minnesota, 2000.

Hagedorn, L. S., Nora A., and Pascarella, E. T. "Pre-Occupational Segregation Among First-Year College Students: An Application of the Duncan Dissimilarity Index." *Journal of College Student Development,* 1996, *37*(4), 425–437.

Hall, R., and Sandler, B. (). "The Classroom Climate: A Chilly One for Women?" Project on the Status and Education of Women. Washington, D.C.: Association of American Colleges, 1982.

Laden, B. V. "The Educational Pipeline: Organizational and Protective Factors Influencing the Academic Progress of Hispanic Community College Students with Potential At Risk Characteristics." Unpublished Ph.D. dissertation, Stanford University, 1994.

Laden, B. V. "Celebratory Socialization of Culturally Diverse Students Through Academic and Support Services." In K. M. Shaw, J. R. Valadez, and R. A. Rhoads (eds.), *Community Colleges as Cultural Texts.* New York: State University of New York Press, 1999, pp. 173–194.

Laden, B. V., and Hagedorn, L. S. "Job Satisfaction Among Faculty of Color in Academe: Individual Survivors or Institutional Transformers?" In L. S. Hagedorn (Ed.), *What Contributes to Job Satisfaction Among Faculty and Staff.* New Directions for Institutional Research, no. 105. San Francisco: Jossey-Bass, 2000.

Laden, B. V., and Turner, C.S.V. "Viewing Community College Students Through the Lenses of Gender and Color." In B. K. Townsend (ed.), *Gender and Power in the Community College.* New Directions for Community Colleges, no. 89. San Francisco: Jossey-Bass, 1995.

Morrison, A. M., White, R. P., Van Velsor, E. and The Center for Creative Leadership. *Breaking the Glass Ceiling: Can Women Reach the Top of America's Largest Corporations?* Reading, Mass.: Addison-Wesley, 1987.

National Center for Education Statistics. "Postsecondary Education." *Digest of Education Statistics, 2000.* Washington, D.C.: U.S. Government Printing Office, 2000.

National Center for Education Statistics (2000), "Instructional Faculty and Staff in Public 2-year Colleges" (NCES 2000–192), Washington, D.C.: U.S. Department of Education, 2001.

Rendón, L. I. *Chicanos in South Texas Community Colleges: A Study of Student Institutional-Related Determinants of Educational Outcomes.* Unpublished Ph.D. dissertation, University of Michigan, 1982.

Rendón, L. I. "From the Barrio to the Academy: Revelations of a Mexican American "Scholarship Girl." In L. S. Zwerling and H. London (eds.), *First-Generation Students: Confronting the Cultural Issues.* New Directions for Community Colleges, no. 80. San Francisco: Jossey-Bass, 1992.

Tabachnick, B. G., and Fidell, L. S. *Using Multivariate Statistics.* New York: HarperCollins, 1996.

Townsend, B. K. "Women Community College Faculty: On the Margins or in the Mainstream?" In B. K. Townsend (ed.), *Gender and Power in the Community College.* New Directions for Community Colleges, no. 89. San Francisco: Jossey-Bass, 1995, pp. 39–46.

Turner, C.S.V. "Organizational Determinants of the Transfer of Hispanic Students from Two- to Four-Year Colleges." Unpublished Ph.D. dissertation, Stanford University, 1988.

Twombly, S. B. "Gendered Images of Community College Leadership: What Messages They Send." In B. K. Townsend (ed.), *Gender and Power in the Community College.* New Directions for Community Colleges, no. 89. San Francisco: Jossey-Bass, 1995.

U.S. Department of Commerce, "Profiles of General Demographic Characteristics: 2000 Census of Population and Housing," May 2001. [http://www.census.gov/Press Release/www/2001/2khus.pdf]

Vetter, B. M. "What Is Holding Up the Glass Ceiling? Barriers to Women in the Science and Engineering Workforce." Occasional Paper 92–3. Washington, D.C.: Commission on Professionals in Science and Technology, 1992.

Weis, L. "Discordant Voices in the Community Colleges." In L. S. Zwerling and H. London (eds.), *First-Generation Students: Confronting the Cultural Issues.* New Directions for Community Colleges, no. 80. San Francisco: Jossey-Bass, 1992.

Wilson, R. "An MIT Professor's Suspicion of Bias Leads to a New Movement for Academic Women." *Chronicle of Higher Education.* December 3, 1999.

Wood, J. T. *Gendered Lives.* Belmont, Calif.: Wadsworth, 1997.

LINDA SERRA HAGEDORN *is an associate professor at the Rossier School of Education at the University of Southern California, the associate director of the Center for Higher Education Policy Analysis, and the program chair of the Community College Leadership Program.*

BERTA VIGIL LADEN *is an associate professor in the Department of Theory and Policy Studies in Education at the Ontario Institute for Studies in Education at the University of Toronto.*

8

Minority faculty voice their views on a variety of issues through both quantitative and qualitative data, revealing issues of concern and areas of satisfaction.

Campus Life for Faculty of Color: Still Strangers After All These Years?

Beverly L. Bower

The cultural changes of the 1960s and early 1970s, which occurred as a result of the Civil Rights movement, the War on Poverty, and the women's movement, diversified America's college campuses. Since that time, higher education institutions have consistently measured the size of ethnic minority populations of students, faculty, and staff on America's campuses. These studies have shown that ethnic minority student populations at four-year colleges and universities have risen from 13.4 percent in 1976 to 23.7 percent in 1997 (National Center for Education Statistics, 2000). Ethnic minorities represent a larger percentage of the student population at community colleges than they do at four-year colleges and universities. Open-access admission, accessibility of location, and availability of short-term vocational programs have made community colleges attractive to many minority students, both urban and rural. Statistics continue to indicate that community colleges have become the access point for minority students seeking a college education. National Center for Education Statistics (NCES) data show that the percentage of minority students in two-year colleges has risen during the last twenty-five years from 19.8 percent in 1976 to 31.8 percent in 1997, with much of this change attributable to Hispanic and Asian student populations (NCES, 2000).

The importance of a minority faculty campus presence for the increasing population of ethnic minority students is discussed in numerous sources. Data on community college faculty, including statistics on the minority faculty population, have been gathered by NCES, the Higher Education Research Institute, the Carnegie Foundation for the Advancement of Teaching, and others. A review of the number of minority community college faculty over the last thirty years shows a substantial increase from 1.6

percent in 1968 to 14.1 percent in 1998 (NCES, 2001; Olivas, 1979). However these figures also indicate a continued underrepresentation of this population.

The literature on community college minority faculty emphasizes recruitment and retention. Numerous works have been written over the last twenty to thirty years about the programs, methods, and initiatives devised to attract and retain ethnic minority faculty. Case studies abound; national surveys have been conducted to gather information from college administrators regarding efforts along these lines as part of strategies to diversify campuses. However, qualitative data gathered directly from minority community college faculty are scarce. An exception is *In the Words of the Faculty* by Earl Seidman (1985). This book is based on research from two qualitative studies of community college faculty and includes a chapter written from in-depth interviews of minority faculty in New York and California.

Seidman states that the minority faculty he interviewed, whether in New York or California, describes similar experiences and raises concerns about similar issues. He concludes that "the minority faculty contend with all the issues their non-minority colleagues do, and many more. They must also face issues of racism in their everyday work" (p. 209). To examine characteristics and experiences of current community college minority faculty, the study in this chapter used quantitative data from the recent Center for the Study of Community Colleges (CSCC) faculty survey and qualitative data gathered by the author. Although Seidman's interviews were conducted almost twenty years ago, interviews conducted with minority faculty for this chapter yield similar experiences and concerns.

Center for the Study of Community Colleges Faculty Survey

In 2000 the CSCC conducted the most recent national survey of community college faculty (see "Editor's Notes" for more detail on this study's method). This random survey of community college faculty includes 154 individuals (10 percent of the total respondents) identified as ethnic minority (i.e., nonwhite) faculty. Minority respondents consist of seventy-four (4.8 percent of the total respondents) individuals who identify themselves as African-American, thirty (2 percent) as Hispanic, twenty-eight (1.8 percent) as Asian or Pacific Islander, and twenty-two (1.4 percent) as American Indian/Alaskan Native. Most (41.1 percent) of the minority faculty who participated in the survey are forty-five to fifty-four years old; 50 percent are women. Twenty-one percent of the minority faculty in the study have doctoral degrees. An analysis of the responses using statistical measures show that in most respects minority faculty respond to the survey questions similarly to the way nonminority respondents do. Both groups have similar educational backgrounds, career longevity, and involvement in professional associations. However, some differences do emerge.

Careers. Minority respondents are less likely than nonminorities to indicate that their positions involve nonteaching responsibilities. When asked to project their career placement in the year 2005, minority respondents are less likely than nonminorities to think that their current position will be attractive and more likely to think that an administrative position will be attractive. They are also more likely than nonminority faculty to find attractive the prospect of teaching outside of the United States and less likely to consider retirement in the next five years. With most of the minority faculty in the forty-five to fifty-four year old range, it is not surprising to find them considering the possibility of career moves into higher-paying administrative positions, nor would most individuals in this age group be considering retirement in the next five years. As many minority faculty may have family or cultural ties to other countries, the increasing global educational perspective may play a part in the stronger minority interest in teaching outside of the United States.

Professional Development. The survey includes questions relating to professional development activities. Minority faculty are more likely than nonminority faculty to occasionally read discipline-related journals, to subscribe to and read general professional education journals, and to subscribe to and regularly read community college journals. In responding to questions regarding professional development steps they plan to take in the next five years, the largest percentage (37.6 percent) of minorities responding to this question indicate working on a doctorate or some other advanced degree, while the largest percentage (36.8 percent) of nonminorities indicate that their professional development will take place through college in-service opportunities. Minority responses also indicate a closer connection with universities than nonminority faculty in that they have a greater propensity to talk with university colleagues on professional matters and to suggest that students make use of university resources.

Teaching and Curriculum. Their responses to questions about teaching indicate that minority community college faculty are more likely than nonminority faculty to be involved in interdisciplinary team teaching. They are also more likely to have taught honors or remedial courses in the last two years. Survey respondents were also asked to rank the following community college functions: prebaccalaureate transfer, new job-entry skills, remedial education, career skills upgrading, community development, and lifelong learning. With regard to the curricular functions of the community college, minority faculty rate the transfer function as most important, while nonminority faculty rank training for new job-entry skills as most important. New job-entry skills rank second for minority respondents, followed by career skills upgrading, lifelong learning, remedial education, and community development programs, respectively.

Job Satisfaction. In general, both minority and nonminority respondents seem satisfied with their jobs. They give high scores to questions regarding their institutional autonomy and their relationships with students and colleagues. Minority faculty (67 percent) agree overwhelmingly that their colleges provide them with opportunities for professional growth and that given the choice to do it all over again, they would choose the academic life.

Statistical analysis of the data uncovered few differences between the responses of the minority and the nonminority faculty. However, a significant difference between the two groups on a question addressing discrimination on campus leaves the impression that campus life for these groups is not the same. Minority respondents are significantly more likely than nonminority faculty to disagree with the statement that claims of discriminatory practices against women and minority faculty and administrators are greatly exaggerated.

To discover more about the campus life of minority community college faculty, this author visited minority community college faculty on two campuses.

Focus Group Findings

It is informative to hear the voices of minority faculty to capture their experiences in ways that might not be evident in quantitative data. As Krueger (1994, p.19) states, "The focus group presents a more natural environment than that of an individual interview because the participants are influencing and being influenced by others—just as they do in real life." Therefore, focus groups were preferred over individual interviews for this project. While information gathered through this qualitative method is not necessarily generalizable, the consistency of experience within the focus groups at both colleges supports the conclusion that the themes that emerged are not aberrant.

To capture their voices and experiences, minority faculty at two Florida community colleges were asked to participate in focus groups. Both campuses have a predominantly white faculty, staff, and student population. Focus groups included faculty who were Latino and African-American; most were women. They range in community college teaching experience from three years to almost thirty years, with most having experience at only one community college.

Information gathered in the focus groups indicates that some minority community college faculty continue to feel that race or ethnicity influences their interactions with colleagues and students. The focus group discussions were initiated with the question, "What is it like to be a community college faculty member?" From this grand tour question participants explored a number of issues and topics of interest to them. The facilitator interjected only to ask for clarification or to keep the conversation flowing.

The Issue of Race. While conversations at the campuses had different emphases, the issue of race emerged at both sites. Minority faculty express concern about how race/ethnicity influences their reception by colleagues and students. As they recall with some detail encounters they have had over the years with students and faculty alike, it is clear that the experiences of the long-time faculty, many of whom were the among the first minority faculty on their campuses, have made lasting impressions. Isolation, alienation, overt discrimination by peers and students, and a sense of separation are experiences shared by faculty on both campuses.

While stating that she has adjusted to the college now, Libby Alice said she spent the first five years looking for opportunities to leave (pseudonyms are used for all focus group participants). Libby Alice, who comes from a neighboring state, explains why.

> I was the first black professor within the biology department, so maybe that had something to do with it. These students. . . . when they get in a setting where they actually have a minority person over them, they don't appreciate that.
>
> I really didn't have any complaints from the people I worked with, but I got a lot of complaints from students. They were complaining. . . . they couldn't understand my dialect. It seemed like every day somebody was running into my supervisor's office telling him they couldn't understand what I was saying. He was always coming in my office and I just felt. . . . he was telling me one thing and the students something else, and it bothered me.

Victoria, who started teaching at the community college in 1978, recalls encounters with colleagues who publicly discounted and devalued her input.

> I found that kind of racist mentality not just from the students, but sometimes from "bosses." I have been put down, even at meetings. We were talking in an English [department] meeting about verb uses, including the passive voice, for a final exam. And they said, "Well, we don't need to include it in the final exam." When I said, "Well, why not?" The chairman said, "How would you know? You're Hispanic." Then he said something like I probably didn't even know what the passive voice was.

She expresses the pain of these early encounters:

> It would take. . . . an iron shield to stop from hurting from all the slices and put downs. You get to the point where you don't even contribute anymore, because you're looked down upon. [As though] "What do you have to contribute here?"

While more recent hires may not experience overt racism by students and faculty, their interactions, with students in particular, indicate that race still has a negative effect on their professional well-being. As Dora summed up the discussion of student assumptions about minority faculty, faculty around the table nodded and quietly vocalized their agreement:

Let me tell you what the two views are in the very beginning. The first, from the white, is that she's black, she probably doesn't know what she's talking about. Even when your credentials are right there with the best of them, and sometimes better than others. The black ones assume some kind of bond because you're "sister-girl," you know, and so [think they] can get away with anything.

Minority faculty perceive that race can affect their relationships with both white and minority students. While white students may harbor doubts about the expertise of minority faculty, minority students may assume that shared ethnic bonds will lead to special liberties.

And although race may be an aspect influencing *their* campus interactions, they are aware that race is not an issue with which their nonminority colleagues must cope. Howard describes the perceptions of the minority faculty in the focus groups, when he states:

They [i.e., white faculty] very seldom think about race. We think about it all the time. . . . It may not be to a point where we're consumed or with a chip on our shoulders, but it's a part of our every day life. Whatever we do, wherever we go.

Just as the minority respondents in the CSCC survey indicated more awareness of discrimination on campus, the focus group faculty recognizes that minority status is a factor in their campus lives.

Student Quality. The other issue that emerged on both campuses was concern for student quality. A number of the focus group faculty indicate a perceived change in the quality of the general student population. The following statements illustrate their concern.

I [have] concern myself about the black students that we get here. I don't feel that we recruit enough quality minority students. I think we should be recruiting quality, period.

Students in general are changing, not just the level of ability has changed, to me, dramatically. The whole purpose of why they're here seems to be lost, you know. The students aren't here for the reasons I think they should be. . . . They come to college naturally for an education, but some come to college for the paper. They come for the degree, but they're not really prepared to put forth effort, and the time, and the dedication. . . . It becomes frustrating for those of us who have not changed with them.

This perceived change in student quality can put stress on the conscientious faculty member, as Dora expresses:

I get frustrated because that's what makes work for me. When I go in prepared and I've assigned a reading. You're supposed to read this so we can discuss it. Then I find that I'm talking to two people and the rest of them don't have a clue about what the story was about or what the assignment was about. That's frustrating to me because I've got to figure out, ok, what can I do now to overcome this?

Job Satisfaction. These faculty have, however, found ways to cope with the frustrations of campus life. The discussions reveal coping strategies and positives of working as community college faculty. Although she has had some difficult times on her campus, Victoria says that she has survived because she believes she can make a difference in the lives of her students:

[I]concentrate on what I'm doing and the success I have. I have a lot of students that start out with a negative attitude. Eventually they go to the universities and then, years later, they will either call me or come see me or write to me and tell me how much I have contributed. They have realized that I did make a difference in their lives. That's something that has kept me going.

Portia, who is planning to get her doctorate and has been contemplating the opportunities it will provide, puts it this way:

I've been thinking about teaching at a four-year institution. But I like the makeup of this place. I like the fact that you have people who are here who have been told, "You'll never make it." They come from broken families. There are single mothers here. Women whose husbands are alcoholics. There's the diversity of the age here. I love it. I wouldn't change that because that's what keeps it interesting.

Others talk about the freedom of faculty life. While in some ways this life is more structured than several participants would prefer, in general they enjoy the flexibility in scheduling courses and the variety of classes. Dora expresses the general feelings of her colleagues:

I think that we're lucky here at [this college] in a lot of ways. I complain just like the average person, but you know the bottom line is that we are lucky. I've talked to people at [the local university] and I have a friend who works down at [another university] and, you know, when you start comparing things, they're surprised at the freedom [we have here].

These statements and others made by the focus group participants echo the appreciation for autonomy and general satisfaction with community college faculty life that minority respondents to the CSCC survey express.

Summary

Themes in the conversations of the focus groups complement findings of the CSCC study regarding the attitudes and experiences of minority community college faculty. Responses of minority faculty in the focus groups and the CSCC survey indicate awareness of discrimination on campus. Focus group faculty discussed personal encounters with discrimination, while minority faculty perceived the presence of discriminatory practices on campus significantly more than nonminority faculty. Minority faculty in the survey and the focus groups express concerns about student quality and preparedness for college-level work. Faculty in the focus groups discussed a decrease in the level of student ability over the years and 59 percent of the minority faculty in the survey agreed with the statement, "Students are not as well prepared as they were five years ago."

While discrimination and student quality may be concerns for minority faculty, both the focus group faculty and the minority faculty surveyed by CSCC express general satisfaction with their professional lives. Focus group faculty talked about the flexibility and freedom of community college faculty life and the rewards in seeing students progress toward their goals. Minority faculty survey responses indicate similar attitudes about the quality of faculty life. The large majority rate aspects of faculty life excellent or good when asked about autonomy (90 percent), opportunities to be creative (84 percent), and general working environment (79 percent). Responses to these questions and other questions indicate strong job satisfaction among minority faculty. The data gathered by survey and focus groups describe similar perceptions of campus climate for minority community college faculty.

Conclusion

Community colleges are an important sector of American higher education. As U.S. minority populations grow, community college minority student populations will expand. As the U.S. population ages, community college faculty retirements will increase. These factors presage a continuing increase in minority faculty on community college campuses. The CSCC survey and the focus groups provide only snapshots of the lives and experiences of community college minority faculty. National trend data for this population are limited. Analysis of the CSCC data uncovers few areas where minority faculty responses differ from nonminority responses, because the CSCC study was not designed to address subtle issues and contexts of campus life. However, differences between minority and nonminority faculty on key campus climate questions in the CSCC study echo the experiences revealed in the minority faculty focus groups. Nevertheless, the picture remains incomplete. What Carter and Ottinger (1992, p. 8) stated conclusively almost ten years ago remains true: "Ongoing data collection efforts concerning faculty are needed, particularly in a time when colleges may be faced with critical faculty shortages. More data are needed to monitor the experiences of minority faculty."

References

Carter, D. J., and Ottinger, C. A. "Community College Faculty: A Profile." *Research Briefs*, 3(7). Washington, D.C.: American Council on Education, Division of Policy Analysis and Research, 1992. (ED352 095)

Krueger, R. *Focus Groups: A Practical Guide for Applied Research.* Newbury Park, Calif.: Sage, 1994.

National Center for Education Statistics. *Background Characteristics, Work Activities, and Compensation of Faculty and Instructional Staff in Postsecondary Institutions: Fall, 1998.* Washington, D.C.: Author, 2001. Retrieved July 6, 2001 from [http://nces.ed.gov/fast-facts/ display.asp?id=61].

National Center for Education Statistics. *Digest of Education Statistics, 1999.* Washington, D.C.: Author, 2000. Retrieved July 9, 2001, from [http://www.nces.ed .gov/ pubsearch/pubsinfo.asp?pubid=2000031].

Olivas, M. A. *The Dilemma of Access: Minorities in Two Year Colleges.* Washington, D.C.: Howard University Press, 1979.

Seidman, E. *In the Words of the Faculty: Perspectives on Improving Teaching and Educational Quality in Community Colleges.* San Francisco: Jossey-Bass, 1985.

BEVERLY L. BOWER *is assistant professor in the Higher Education Program and research director of the Hardee Center for Women in Higher Education at Florida State University, Tallahassee.*

This chapter provides a brief overview of the history of faculty development efforts at community colleges and a summary of the research. The chapter also discusses how community colleges can implement a successful faculty development program.

The Current State of Faculty Development in Two-Year Colleges

John P. Murray

For at least the last third of the twentieth century, community colleges have been struggling with the changing demographics that have brought them an increasingly nontraditional student body, one that demands different approaches to teaching and learning than most faculty are prepared for in graduate training. Consequently, from the early days of community colleges, leaders have found it necessary to implement faculty development activities that assist faculty in forming the skills and strategies necessary to provide effective instruction. However, despite devoting considerable resources to this effort, success has been quite limited (Maxwell and Kazlauskas, 1992).

The purpose of this chapter is to provide a brief overview of the history of faculty development efforts at community colleges and to summarize research findings that might help us understand why these costly efforts have produced only meager results. The chapter also discusses how community colleges can implement a successful faculty development program.

The Roots of Faculty Development in Community Colleges

Prior to the 1970s, faculty development in senior colleges was mostly confined to sabbatical leaves, support to attend discipline-based conferences, visiting professorships, and grants to support research and scholarship (Alstete, 2000). At most community colleges the faculty development involved support only for conference attendance, grants to support innovation in teaching, and, perhaps, sabbatical leaves. Serious efforts to institutionalize faculty development did not take root until the 1970s with the publication of seminal works by Gaff (1975) and Bergquist and Philips (1975). These publications initiated a major paradigm shift—from activities intended to boost the scholarly reputation of professors to multifaceted comprehensive models that included instructional and personal development.

During the 1970s and 1980s, many colleges formalized faculty development programs that focused on three areas: professional development, personal development, and organizational development. Professional development usually included "enabling faculty members to obtain and enhance job-related skills, knowledge, and awareness" (Alstete, 2000, p. iii). Personal development usually included career management and quality of life issues. Organizational development included curriculum and program development. Although the promotional materials sent to faculty contained references to the personal and organizational missions of faculty development, most colleges (especially community colleges) tended to emphasize professional development (i.e., the skills that enabled faculty to do a better job), and this most often meant the improvement of teaching (Schuster, 1990).

Although there have been community colleges since the 1800s, they were not a serious force in higher education until the late 1960s and early 1970s with the exponential growth in both campuses and student enrollment. The mission of the community college was and still is to serve a larger and more educationally diverse student population than that served by four-year institutions. Because community colleges are intended to be the "peoples' colleges" and invite a very heterogeneous and sometimes less academically prepared population to enter through their "open doors," the leaders in the 1960s and 1970s felt the need to "develop" faculty, not only in pedagogy but also in the mission and philosophy of the community college. "A number of faculty development programs center on attitude adjustment—accepting the basic concepts of the community college and its heterogeneous student body. . . ." (Brawer, 1990, p. 51).

Although the rhetoric may have changed, the bedrock philosophical assumption has remained the same—community college students need and deserve a faculty dedicated to teaching all who enter. Faculty must first understand and accept the academic heterogeneity of the student body and then develop diverse pedagogical approaches to enable all to learn. Community college leaders realize that understanding students is a necessary condition for successful teaching. Hence, "attitude adjustment" must play some role in faculty development efforts. If instructional improvement efforts are to succeed, faculty must first accept the unique mission of the community college. That is, faculty should first understand and accept the unique learning differences that exist within the nontraditional population and then be exposed to teaching techniques that match these unique learning styles.

The Status of Faculty Development in Community Colleges Today

An extensive literature review turns up only a few national studies, several statewide or regional studies, and many single-institution studies dealing with faculty development in community colleges. Many of the research studies are over ten years old, and "although some of the regional samples are carefully drawn, the national faculty samples are less adequate" (Maxwell and Kazluasias, 1992, p. 356). Despite some serious methodological questions concerning the existing research, certain themes consistently emerge from the literature:

• Few community colleges make the effort to tie their faculty development programs to the mission of the college.
• Few community colleges attempt to evaluate the success of faculty development programs.
• Faculty participation in most faculty development activities is often minimal, and often those most in need do not participate.

Lack of Goals. The most common thread running through the literature is that most faculty development programs lack goals—especially goals that are tied to the institutional mission. "Although faculty development programs multiplied, basic questions about their focus and purpose often went unanswered" (Brookes and German, 1983, p. 29). Richardson and Moore (1987) argue: "Although organized faculty development occurs at an overwhelming majority of Texas community colleges, there is little evidence that programs are being used as a major instrument for institutional change and improvement that is linked to the accomplishment of college goals' and the establishment of accountability" (p. 29).

Without clear goals tied to institutional plans, faculty development becomes a series of loosely related activities that administrators hope will improve teaching and learning. However, without clear and distinct goals, any improvement is likely to be fleeting and limited in the number of students or faculty it impacts. Articulated goals provide community colleges with a means to work toward lasting changes in teaching and learning. Although goals can change from year to year, they allow the institution to select specific areas (e.g., the use of technology in teaching, writing across the curriculum) for sustained efforts that are much more likely to produce lasting change.

Although there is a dearth of empirical studies on the effectiveness of faculty development, one study does demonstrate that community colleges that link faculty development and institutional goals tend to be more effective educational institutions. Richardson and Wolverton (1994) conclude that "professional development opportunities for faculty members in higher-performing institutions were linked in systematic ways to institutional priorities. In several lower-performing districts, faculty had no clear sense of priorities" (p. 46).

In some ways the failure to tie faculty development to institutional mission is the result of fuzzy thinking on the part of community college leaders (and faculty) over what should be the purpose of faculty development—or, at the very least, over uncertainty about how to achieve their goals. Community college leaders have always recognized that community colleges are vehicles for social justice that can provide educational equity to millions who have been denied it by selective-admission institutions. However, achieving this vision clearly requires radically different approaches to students and teaching at the postsecondary level, for which few new community college faculty have been adequately prepared (Fugate and Amey, 2000). This means that faculty development efforts need to be directed toward assisting faculty in "developing" the teaching skills, and equally important, the "attitude adjustment" that Brawer mentions.

Nonetheless, community college leaders are often caught on the horns of a dilemma. On the one horn, their faculty are often ill-prepared for their role. Often the faculty trained in disciplines at universities do not understand the philosophy and mission of the community college. Consequently, it is not only appropriate for community college leaders to provide development activities that introduce these faculty to the philosophy and mission of the community college but also imperative that they do so.

However, these leaders also face the other horn of the dilemma. They want the respect of traditional higher education institutions. For faculty development, this means adopting the traditional types of programs—e.g., sabbaticals and conference attendance. Moreover, this appears to be what the faculty themselves want (Maxwell and Kazlausias, 1992). The result of this dilemma is a menu of activities from which faculty can choose. However, "we cannot simply assume that menus for individual faculty (voluntary) selections will be adequate or responsive to current or continuing faculty needs" (Clark, Corcoran, and Lewis, 1986, p. 193). The menu of choices needs to be tied directly to the institutional mission. Faculty should be allowed to select from a menu of activities that meet their goals *and* the institution's goals. In this way, both institutions and faculty can grow in ways that ultimately benefit the students they serve.

Lack of Evaluation. Community colleges must assume that their faculty development efforts are in fact effective as there is scant evidence that they attempt to evaluate outcomes. "There is abundant information concerning the structure and organization of professional development. . . . but no data to measure program effectiveness" (Sydow, 2000, p. 383). One national study with 232 community colleges responding found that only 47 percent evaluated faculty development efforts and only 43 percent have evaluation criteria (Grant, 2000). There appear to be two primary reasons for the lack of evaluation. The first goes back to our early concern. "Faculty development is often an ambiguous concept" (Tierney, Ahern, and Kidwell,

1996, p. 38). If we lack clear objectives for faculty development outcomes, how do we measure success? Without a clear idea of where we want to take faculty, it is difficult to know if we have arrived.

We not only lack criteria for measuring effectiveness but also are uncertain about what to measure. "The research is unclear as to which dependent variables in the causal sequence of events must be examined as indicators of program effectiveness: the faculty development programs, the potential changes in teaching behavior, student learning, or some combination of these factors" (Maxwell and Kazlauskas, 1992, p. 355). When community colleges do attempt to assess faculty development, "the methods used to determine effectiveness [are], on the whole, not measures of changes in teacher or student behavior" (Richardson and Moore, 1987, p. 19). For the most part, community college faculty leaders assess only superficial measures of effectiveness such as participants' satisfaction or number of faculty participating in the activities.

The increasing calls by the public for accountability in higher education means that colleges may be called to account for their use of public funds for faculty development. The absence of demonstrable effects on student learning could in fact lead to reduced funding from state governing boards. If so, community college leaders may find themselves unable to defend faculty development expenditures.

Low Faculty Participation. Angelo (1994) succinctly states another theme found in the literature. "First, a relatively small number of faculty take advantage of the programs; second, those faculty who do participate are often the ones who seem to need them least" (p. 3). In what many consider to be the first national study of faculty development in colleges and universities, Centra (1975) reports that "teachers who wanted to get better were the group most involved while those needing improvement seemed the least involved" (p. 59). Nearly twenty years later Maxwell and Kazlausias (1992) draw the same conclusion after reviewing the literature on community colleges' faculty development efforts. "The findings that, thus far, few community college faculty participate effectively in instructional development programs, and the teachers most in need are the least likely to participate. . . . " (p. 351).

What is the cause of this sad state of affairs? Both good teachers and less adequate teachers tend to resent the form faculty development often takes (Brawer, 1990). One community college faculty member states that inservice workshops are "just a total waste of time. Building paper airplanes to promote cooperation and teamwork, listening to a highly paid Ph.D. talk about putting candy on students' desks to raise retention levels, and breaking into little groups to do touchy, feely things are just demeaning and degrading. It's insulting when you think about all the things you could be doing. . . ." (cited in Briggs, 2001).

According to Baldwin and Blackburn (1981) a major reason for the failure of faculty development programs to reach those most in need is that many "faculty development approaches seem to lack a basic understanding of individual professors" (p. 598). That is, administrators of faculty development programs are oblivious to the real needs and desires of faculty. There is certainly evidence to support the view that community college administrators are not in touch with faculty desires. "With 86 percent of the academic instructors desiring further professional development, fewer than 10 percent wanted workshops on their own campuses. In contrast, administrators preferred on-campus workshops and seminars for their instructors, with content centering on pedagogy and community college-related concerns" (Brawer, 1990, p. 51).

The difficulty, however, is that once again we face the horns of the dilemma discussed above. On one horn, we have the desires of the faculty to participate only in activities that further their disciplinary goals and deepen their knowledge of the discipline (Maxwell and Kazausias, 1992). On the other horn, we have the desires of administrators to initiate faculty into the philosophy of the community college so that teaching and learning can be grounded in an understanding of the student. Unfortunately, activities that might help the faculty develop innovative approaches to teaching nontraditional students are the very ones faculty often resent.

Successful Faculty Development in Community Colleges

Although I have focused on the negative aspects of community college faculty development programs, there are numerous examples of successful ones. However, much of the literature describes highly successful, innovative, one-shot programs that are typically limited in duration and scope (Schratz, 1990). Even when such programs are highly successful and lasting, they often do not transfer well to other institutions (Schuster, 1990). Many observers would agree with Schratz's (1990) assessment:

> In many cases so far, activities aimed at improving teaching, and thus trying to answer faculty questions, have had no more than short-term effects. Although these activities aroused faculty interest while underway, they generally failed to prompt instructional staff to reflect on their teaching practices over a longer period of time (p. 99).

Nonetheless, we can learn from these successful programs if we concentrate on the principles on which they are based rather than simply trying to copy the activities. A review of the literature on faculty development and its implications for community colleges suggests that the following are necessary conditions for an effective faculty development program: administrative support that fosters and encourages faculty development, a formalized, structured, goal-directed program, a connection between faculty development and the reward structure, faculty ownership, support from colleagues for investments in teaching, and a belief that good teaching is valued by administrators.

Administrative Support That Fosters and Encourages Faculty Development. The vital importance of leadership from the chief academic officer is the most consistent theme found in the literature, according to Sydow (2000). As Nwagwu says, "The efforts of enhancing teaching effectiveness lie at the door at the college dean. The college dean must provide the leadership for and commitment to improving teaching" (Nwagwu, 1998, p. 13).

The Existence of a Formalized, Structured, and Goal-Directed Development Program. To effect institutional change, faculty development programs must be directly related to the institutional mission and goals (Tierney, Ahern, and Kidwell, 1996), as well as to the goals of individual faculty members. As Vineyard (1994) states, "Some plotted course of improvement rather than either stagnation or mere change for its own sake is desirable. Leadership seeks to stimulate progress, which is change toward carefully considered institutional goals" (p. 370).

Connecting Faculty Development to the Reward Structure. Although all rewards need not be monetary, those who attempt to improve their teaching must be recognized in some way. The recognition might include praise and support for experimentation, even when it fails. Faculty need to know that their efforts are appreciated and that taking a risk is not damaging to their careers. Otherwise, innovation can be stifled (Nwagwu, 1998).

Faculty Ownership. Faculty development programs are more effective when faculty participate in the design and implementation stages. Although faculty need support from academic administrators, they often resist and resent development activities imposed on them. Moreover, research indicates that administrators often misunderstand what faculty believe to be their development needs (Maxwell and Kazlauskas, 1992). Therefore, faculty-driven programs are more likely to be successful.

Colleagues' Support for Investments in Teaching. The respect of and recognition from colleagues is important to most professionals. Because faculty tend to believe that pedagogy is related to discipline, they are more likely to accept pedagogical advice from those within their own disciplines. As noted by Maxwell and Kazlauskas, (1992):

[The] ideal type of consultant is a colleague in one's own department who is an up-to-date specialist in the specific discipline and who also can serve as a model in instructional methods. . . . Surveys of community colleges indicate that expert consultation by colleagues on specific teaching matters. . . . were among. . . . the more effective modes of development (pp. 356–357).

Summary

Faculty development in community colleges is a mixed bag. Numerous examples of effective programs can be found in the literature. However, these programs are short-term and highly idiosyncratic and neither transfer well to other campuses nor have lasting effects. Faculty development programs rarely reach the faculty most in need of assistance and frequently irritate them. They are rarely tied directly to the institution's goals or mission and are not usually evaluated in any meaningful way.

Nonetheless, faculty development programs can be effective and can contribute to the achievement of the overall mission of the community college. To be effective, community college faculty development programs need to be based on sound principles. Effective faculty development programs have administrative support, are formalized, structured, and goal-directed, make a connection between faculty development and the reward structure, have faculty ownership, and are valued by administrators.

References

Alstete, J. W. *Post Tenure Faculty Development: Building a System of Faculty Development Improvement and Appreciation.* ASHE-ERIC Higher Education Report, 27(4). Washington, D.C: George Washington University, 2000.

Angelo, T. "From Faculty Development to Academic Development." *AAHE Bulletin,* June 1994, p. 3.

Baldwin, R. G., and Blackburn, R. T. "The Academic Career as Developmental Process Implications for Higher Education." *Journal of Higher Education,* 1981, 52, 588–614.

Bergquist, W. H., and Philips, S. R. "Components of an Effective Faculty Development Program." *Journal of Higher Education,* 1975, 46, 177–211.

Brawer, F. B. "Faculty Development: The literature: An ERIC Review." *Community College Review,* 1990, 18, 51–56.

Briggs, C. L. "Multicultural Education in the Community College: A Study of Social Science Faculty Perspectives and Practices." Unpublished doctoral dissertation, Texas Tech University, Lubbock, 2001.

Brookes, M.C.T., and German, K. L. "Meeting the Challenges: Developing Faculty Careers." ASHE-ERIC Higher Education Research Report, no. 3. Washington, D.C.: Association for the Study of Higher Education, 1983.

Centra, J. A. *Faculty Development Practices in U.S. Colleges and Universities.* Princeton, N.J.: Educational Testing Service. 1975.

Clark, S. M., Corcoran, M. E., and Lewis, D. R. "The Case for an Institutional Perspective on Faculty Development." *Journal of Higher Education,* 1986, 57, 176–195.

Fugate, A. L., and Amey, M. J. "Career Stages of Community College Faculty: A Qualitative Analysis of Their Career Paths, Roles, and Development." *Community College Review,* 2000, 28, 1–22.

Gaff J. G. *Toward Faculty Renewal: Advances in Faculty Instructional and Organizational Development.* San Francisco: Jossey-Bass, 1975.

Grant, M. R. "Faculty Development at Publicly Supported Two-Year Colleges." Paper presented at 42nd annual conference of the Council for the Study of Community Colleges. Washington, D.C., April 2000.

Maxwell, W. E., and Kazlauskas, E. J. "Which Faculty Development Methods Really Work in Community Colleges? A Review of the Research." *Community/Junior College Quarterly,* 1992, *16,* 351–360.

Nwagwu, E. C. "How Community College Administrators Can Improve Teaching Effectiveness." *Community College Journal of Research,* 1998, *22,* 11–19.

Richardson, R., and Moore, W. "Faculty Development and Evaluation in Texas Community Colleges." *Community/Junior College Quarterly,* 1987, *11,* 19–32.

Richardson, R. C., Jr., and Wolverton M. "Leadership Strategies." In A. M. Cohen and F. Brawer (eds.), *Managing Community Colleges: A Handbook for Effective Practice.* San Francisco: Jossey-Bass, 1994.

Schratz, M. "Researching While Teaching: A Collaborative Action Research Model to Improve College Teaching." *Journal on Excellence in College Teaching,* 1990, *1,* 98–108.

Schuster, J. H., and others. *Enhancing Faculty Careers: Strategies for Development and Renewal.* San Francisco: Jossey-Bass, 1990.

Sydow, D. "Long-Term Investment in Professional Development: Real Dividends in Teaching and Learning." *Community College Journal of Research and Practice,* 2000, *24,* 383–397.

Tierney, W. G., Ahern, B., and Kidwell, C. S. "Enhancing Faculty Development at Tribal Colleges." *Tribal College Journal,* Winter 1996, pp. 36–39.

Vineyard, E. E. "The Administrator's Role in Staff Management. In A. M. Cohen and F. Brawer (eds.), *Managing Community Colleges: A Handbook for Effective Practice.* San Francisco: Jossey-Bass, 1994.

JOHN P. MURRAY is an associate professor of community leadership at Texas Tech University. He had a twenty-five-year career in community college teaching and administration before joining the Texas Tech faculty.

10

Feedback from faculty indicates that community colleges are still struggling to create of a sense of community. Drawing from the literature, the authors discuss the challenges to community college faculty's sense of belonging and recommend ways to address five critical factors of community building.

Building Community: The Second Century, the Same Challenge

Iris M. Weisman and John W. Marr, Jr.

The occasion of the one hundredth birthday of the community college in America has prompted much reflection on this institution's past, celebration of its present, and forecasting about its future. In the language of learning organizations, there is little doubt that the community college is "continually expanding its capacity to create its future" (Senge, 1990, p.14). Part of the long-term success of community colleges is certainly attributable to the dynamic nature of the institution's mission.

While many have expressed concern about the ever-expanding nature of the community college mission, Bailey and Averianova (1998) note that "community colleges are probably not going to significantly restrict their activities. There is too much enthusiasm and political support for many of their new functions and the trend in the last decades has clearly been towards comprehensiveness" (p. 29). Unfortunately, an expanding mission presents significant challenges to current administrative structures, campus cultures, and individual work relationships. At the top of the list of challenges for community colleges is the charge to redefine community "not only as a region to be served, but also as a climate to be created" (Commission on the Future of Community Colleges, 1988, p. 3). There are indications that building this climate has not occurred, prompting one author to assert that community colleges indeed "lack a sense of community" (Mittelstet, 1994, p. 550).

Central to establishing the college as community is to understand the factors that affect faculty's sense of community. "Faculty are the front-line forces, interacting directly with students in the teaching and learning processes. All other [community] college services are in a sense supportive of this academic thrust" (Vineyard, 1994, p. 379). This chapter will focus on one characteristic of community, the sense of belonging (Gardner, 1991, p. 18) and how to foster a sense of community for and with faculty.

Factors Affecting a Sense of Belonging

Of the myriad factors that affect faculty's sense of belonging, we have limited our discussion to five areas: the academic hierarchy, satisfaction with interpersonal relations, degree of autonomy, orientation to the institution, and opportunities for professional development. We have incorporated data from the Center for the Study of Community Colleges (CSCC) study in as many of these areas as possible. (Please see "Editor's Notes" for more information about this study.)

The Academic Hierarchy. The positioning of the community college within higher education and the growth and bureaucratization of community colleges place community college professionals at the bottom rungs of the academic hierarchy. By offering accessible and affordable education, community colleges serve students who would not be accepted by other colleges and universities. Community colleges provide lower-division undergraduate education, vocational training, and personal growth opportunities, thus placing themselves at the bottom of the higher education hierarchy. The different educational requirements for community college faculty and the lack of emphasis on faculty-conducted research also place community colleges "lower" in this pecking order.

Seidman (1985) contends that an academic hierarchy exists within community colleges as well. For example, women and minority faculty have lower positions hierarchically than do white male faculty, and occupational faculty are considered lower hierarchically than academic faculty. Adjunct faculty, regardless of discipline or field, find themselves at the very bottom.

The net result of the academic hierarchy is a proliferation of divisiveness, competition, and the accentuation of differences instead of commonalities. These outcomes, obviously, are not conducive to developing and maintaining a sense of belonging.

Are Seidman's findings from 1985 outdated? Sadly, they do not appear to be. (See, for example, Hagedorn and Laden's discussion of women community college faculty in Chapter Seven, Bower's presentation of the experiences and perceptions of community college faculty of color in Chapter Eight, and Gappa and Leslie's comparison of community college and four-year part-time faculty in Chapter Six.)

In a study involving 266 community college faculty, Townsend and LaPaglia (2000) find that community college faculty believe that "four-year college and university faculty consider [community college faculty] to be on the margins of higher education" (p. 46). However, one positive finding of this study is that community college faculty members do not hold the same perception of themselves. Townsend and LaPaglia's (2000) findings shed light on several studies that have documented that community college faculty generally enjoy high levels of job satisfaction (Hutton and Jobe, 1985; Milosheff, 1990; Truell, Price, and Joyner, 1998). One study, conducted among secondary, community college, and four-year college faculty, documents that among the three groups, community college faculty exhibit the highest levels of job satisfaction. This study notes that "perhaps these teachers have found the community college to be the right 'fit' in meeting their personal and professional needs" (Riday, Bingham, and Harvey, 1985, p. 47). These and other studies have also reported on the variety of factors that play a role in determining the relative level of job satisfaction among community college faculty. Of particular importance for the CSCC study is the information provided by these studies on the critical role of interpersonal relationships in the lives of faculty members.

Satisfaction with Interpersonal Relations. Research on community college faculty job satisfaction consistently indicates that satisfaction with the work itself (such as teaching and working directly with students) is the strongest variable in determining overall job satisfaction (Hill, 1986; Hutton and Jobe, 1985; Riday, Bingham, and Harvey, 1985; Truell, Price, and Joyner, 1998). These same data also consistently indicate that relationships with peers and supervisors are very important in determining overall job satisfaction.

Research conducted among community college administrators draws similar conclusions on the importance of interpersonal relationships with faculty (Murray and Murray, 1998; Seagren and others, 1994). The shared perception of the contribution of positive interpersonal relationships to faculty job satisfaction highlights the significance of findings below.

In the CSCC study, 92 percent of the full-time faculty and 91 percent of the part-time faculty state that their relationships with colleagues are either good or excellent. When asked how much time faculty spend with their colleagues in informal interactions, 56 percent of the faculty (62 percent of the full-time faculty and 42 percent of the part-time faculty) responded that on their most recent working day they spent one hour per day in informal interactions. A small percentage spent more time together: approximately 13 percent of both the full-time and the part-time faculty spent two or more hours together in informal interactions on their most recent working day.

Furthermore, there are clear indications that at least some faculty would enjoy more opportunities to sustain these relationships. More than one-third of all faculty (38 percent) state that they would prefer to spend more hours per day in informal interaction with colleagues. Of the faculty who had spent one hour per day with colleagues in informal interaction, 45 percent indicate that they would prefer to spend more time in this activity. Of the faculty who spent two or more hours per day with colleagues in informal interaction, 27 percent indicate that they would prefer to spend more time in this activity.

Formal interaction with faculty is also valued. Slightly more than one-fifth (22 percent) of all faculty (24 percent of the full-time faculty and 15 percent of the part-time faculty) have taught courses jointly with faculty outside of their departments. Moreover, 38 percent of the full-time faculty and 42 percent of the part-time faculty state that their courses would improve through more interaction with colleagues or administrators.

Of the faculty in the CSCC study who state that the courses they teach could be improved by more interaction with colleagues or administrators, 46 percent rate the advice on teaching from department chairs as being quite useful, 65 percent rate the advice on teaching from colleagues as being quite useful, and 19 percent rate the advice on teaching from administrators as being quite useful.

Faculty are satisfied with their relationship with administrators, as well. Approximately 75 percent of the full-time faculty and 83 percent of the part-time faculty (78 percent of all faculty) rate their relationship with administrators as being good or excellent.

We believe that the CSCC data indicate that community college faculty are relatively satisfied with their interpersonal relationships at work. This finding is particularly important because, as stated above, faculty's satisfaction with personal relationships enhances their job satisfaction and sense of community.

Degree of Autonomy. Since community college faculty focus their work around teaching and learning (as opposed to research and publication), the classroom represents "a refuge, where the instructor still maintains a certain sense of sovereignty" (White, 1991, p. 113). Indeed, in the CSCC study, 92 percent of the full-time faculty and 96 percent of the part-time faculty rate their degree of autonomy as being excellent or good. Likewise, 90 percent of the full-time faculty and 69 percent of the part-time faculty rate the freedom to choose textbooks and other instructional materials in their areas as being good or excellent.

Although, from these results, it is clear that community college faculty appreciate the freedom to teach without administrative interference, this autonomy may lead to a fragmented faculty, who generally are not expected to work together. In a study of approximately 260 community college instructors (Grubb, 1999), one faculty member states that community college faculty are "wrapped up in [their] individual work. . . . I'm not sure what collegiality would be based on" (p. 285). Thus academic freedom and the lack of collaboration may also be responsible for creating a sense of isolation among community college faculty.

Community colleges cannot thrive if their faculty feel isolated from one another and from the institution. Community colleges are "made up of *relationships* between the various parties; the parts are not actually separate and distinct but instead intermingling; they are water from several glasses flowing together in a pool" (Cain, 1999, p. 122). One important strategy to address the sense of isolation is the implementation of a strong faculty orientation program.

Orientation to the Institution. In any organization, formal employee orientation programs provide management's first opportunity to impart a sense of the institution's values and culture. An orientation program is the community college's opportunity to welcome new faculty to its community, provide faculty with basic institutional and employment information, and to begin the process of socializing, inducting, and initiating (Tucker, 1993) the faculty into the organization. In the CSCC study, barely half (49 percent) of all respondents state that a formal orientation program was available to them when they were hired by their CSCC community college. These faculty represent 49 percent of the full-time faculty and 51 percent of the part time faculty.

Of all CSCC respondents, 38 percent of the faculty strongly or somewhat agree that their community college does too little to orient new faculty. Of the 721 faculty who have an orientation program available to them, one-fifth strongly or somewhat agree that their community college does too little to orient new faculty. Moreover, of the 741 faculty who did not have an orientation program available to them when they were hired, slightly more than half (54 percent) strongly or somewhat agree that their community college does too little to orient new faculty. From the faculty's perspective (as well as ours), these statistics represent a failing on the part of community colleges.

Opportunities for Professional Development. The opportunity to increase knowledge and develop skills while employed leads to an improved sense of belonging. "You cannot separate building community from building individuals" (Shaffer and Anundsen, 1993, p. 119). In the CSCC study, only 39 percent of all respondents strongly agree that their institution provides them with continuing professional stimulation and growth. In addition, 60 percent of all faculty state that their institution should expand its professional development opportunities, such as providing seminars on issues in teaching. Approximately 82 percent of the full-time and 74 percent of the part-time faculty strongly or somewhat agree that most faculty should participate in some type of academic coursework or creative activity every three years.

In fact, 83 percent of the full-time and 77 percent of the part-time faculty who participated in the CSCC study state that they "would like to take steps toward professional development in the next five years." The survey lists four professional development activities: of taking inservice courses at their college, enrolling in courses at a university, earning a master's degree, and of earning a Ph.D., Ed.D., or terminal degree. Faculty were asked to identify the professional development activity that most appealed to them. Table 10.1 shows the percentage of faculty who state that they would like to participate in the above-mentioned professional development activities over the next five years.

Three of the four professional development activities were selected as top choices in fairly comparable amounts. The most frequently selected activity was taking inservice courses at their college (27 percent). The next appealing activity was earning a Ph.D., Ed.D., or other terminal degree (22 percent). Following close behind was enrolling in courses at a university

**Table 10.1. Faculty Interest in Professional Development
Opportunities**

	All Faculty n = 1531	Full-time Faculty n = 1064	Part-time Faculty n = 467
Take inservice courses at their college	27%	28%	23%
Enroll in courses at a university	20%	23%	15%
Earn a master's degree	9%	7%	12%
Earn a Ph.D., Ed.D., or other advanced degree	22%	21%	24%

(20 percent). Earning a master's degree was the least appealing choice
(9 percent).

That earning a master's degree was the least appealing activity is not
surprising as nearly all faculty (79 percent) have at least a master's degree.
Almost 16 percent of the faculty have earned doctorates and 65 percent have
earned a master's degree as their highest degree. In addition, another 10
percent of the faculty are working either on a master's or doctoral degree.
We believe that it is the institution's obligation to ensure that the professional development needs of faculty are met. (See Murray's analysis of the
current state of faculty development and his synthesis of the necessary components of an effective faculty development program in Chapter Nine.)
Furthermore, by paying attention to all five above-mentioned factors (academic hierarchy, interpersonal relations, degree of autonomy, orientation
to the institution, and opportunities for professional development), a greater
sense of belonging to the college as community will be achieved.

Implications for Building Community

"The best [community colleges] have administrators who are committed to
teaching and who have managed to orient every single policy in their colleges
toward the improvement of teaching" (Grubb, 1999, p. 302). We believe that
an essential component of an institution's efforts toward improving teaching
is the building of community among and between faculty and the community
college. Although the CSCC study reveals that faculty's satisfaction with interpersonal relations is relatively strong, the other factors are not shown to be
well addressed by community colleges or are not part of the study. Therefore,
we offer as concluding remarks these strategies for building community.

Academic hierarchy: Boost faculty's pride in the unique role of community
colleges and the need for diverse programs of study.

- Provide opportunities for faculty and staff to learn about the mission of
  the community college and celebrate its important role for community
  well-being.
- Provide a forum for academic and career-oriented faculty alike to share
  professional accomplishments and contributions to the institution.

Interpersonal Relations: Continue to provide faculty with opportunities to interact with other faculty and administrators.

- Set aside time for faculty to meet with their colleagues within their disciplines.
- Provide faculty with reliable access to the Internet and develop electronic forums for building community in cyberspace.
- Assist faculty in developing collegial relationships despite the limitations of incompatible work schedules and geography.

Degree of Autonomy: Enhance academic autonomy by developing a supportive academic infrastructure.

- Work to ensure that all institutional policies and procedures support high-quality teaching and learning, thus supporting faculty and their contribution to the institution.
- Ensure that all faculty have office space for meeting with students, institutional e-mail accounts or telephone numbers for communication with students and colleagues, and access to departmental resources.

Orientation to the Institution: Make sure that part-time and full-time faculty understand the context in which they work.

- Establish orientation programs for faculty, and compensate them for attending these sessions.
- Establish mentoring or peer partnering programs to assist newer faculty in becoming socialized to community colleges, community college teaching, and their discourse community.

Professional Development: Encourage lifelong learning, keeping current in one's field, and enhancing one's teaching and learning strategies.

- Establish Faculty Development Days with a variety of activities that will attract participation from a diverse group of faculty.
- Include external professional development activities as part of faculty's professional responsibilities.

Building and maintaining community for community college faculty cannot be overemphasized. Although college administrators must understand their primary responsibility for building community, all academic leaders—administrators and faculty alike—must work together to establish a "web of mutual connection" (Shaffer and Anundsen, 1993, p. xiv) in supporting teaching, learning, and one another within the community college.

References

Bailey, T. R., and Averianova, I. E. *Multiple Missions of Community Colleges: Conflicting or Complementary?* New York: Community College Research Center, 1998.

Cain, M. S. *The Community College in The Twenty-First Century: A Systems Approach.* Lanham, Md.: University Press of America, 1999.

Commission on the Future of Community Colleges. *Building Communities: A Vision for a New Century.* Washington, D.C.: American Association of Community and Junior Colleges, 1988.

Gardner, J. W. *Building Community.* Washington, D.C.: Independent Sector, 1991.

Grubb, W. N. *Honored but Invisible: An Inside Look at Teaching in Community Colleges.* New York: Routledge, 1999.

Hill, E. A. "Job Satisfaction Facets as Predictors of Commitment to or Withdrawal from the Work Organization Among Selected Community College Faculty in New York State." *Community/Junior College Quarterly,* 1986, *10,* 1–11.

Hutton, J. B., and Jobe, M. E. "Job Satisfaction of Community College Faculty." *Community/Junior College Quarterly of Research and Practice,* 1985, *9*(4), 317–324.

Milosheff, E. "Factors Contributing to Job Satisfaction at the Community College." *Community College Review,* *18*(1), 1990, 12–22.

Mittelstet, S. K. "A Synthesis of the Literature on Understanding the New Vision for Community College Culture: The Concept of Community Building." In G. A. Baker, III (ed.), *A Handbook on the Community College in America: Its History, Mission, and Management.* Westport, Conn.: Greenwood Press, 1994.

Murray, J. P., and Murray, J. I. "Job Satisfaction and the Propensity to Leave an Institution Among Two-Year College Division Chairpersons." *Community College Review,* 1998, *25*(4), 45–59.

Riday, G. E., Bingham, R. D., and Harvey, T. R. "Satisfaction of Community College Faculty: Exploding a Myth." *Community College Review,* 1985, *12*(3), 46–50.

Seagren, A. L., and others. *Academic Leadership in Community Colleges.* Lincoln: University of Nebraska Press, 1994.

Seidman, E. *In the Words of the Faculty.* San Francisco: Jossey-Bass, 1985.

Senge, P. M. *The Fifth Discipline: The Art and Practice of the Learning Organization.* New York: Currency Doubleday, 1990.

Shaffer, C. R., and Anundsen, K. *Creating Community Anywhere: Finding Support and Connection in a Fragmented World.* New York: Tarcher/Perigee, 1993.

Townsend, B. K., and LaPaglia, N. "Are We Marginalized Within Academe? Perceptions of Two-Year College Faculty." *Community College Review,* 2000, *27*(1), 41–48.

Truell, A. D., Price, W. T., Jr., and Joyner, R. L. "Job Satisfaction Among Community College Occupational-Technical Faculty." *Community College Journal of Research and Practice,* 1998, *22*(2), 111–122.

Tucker, A. *Chairing the Academic Department: Leadership Among Peers.* Phoenix: American Council on Education and Oryx Press, 1993.

Vineyard, E. E. "The Administrator's Role in Staff Development." In A. M. Cohen, and F. B. Brawer (eds.), *Managing Community Colleges: A Handbook for Effective Practice.* San Francisco: Jossey-Bass, 1994.

White, K. B. "The Implementation of State-Mandated Program Review: A Case Study of Governance and Decision-Making in Community Colleges." Unpublished doctoral dissertation, University of Arizona, 1991.

IRIS M. WEISMAN is associate professor of higher education and chair, Community College Management, at Antioch University–McGregor in Yellow Spring, Ohio.

JOHN W. MARR, JR., is dean of career and technical programs at Columbus State Community College in Columbus, Ohio.

11

In this chapter, relevant research literature and results from the Center for the Study of Community Colleges (CSCC) study are used to explore the development of a professional identity for community college faculty.

Toward a Professionalized Community College Professoriate

Charles L. Outcalt

As many chapters in this volume demonstrate, results from the 2000 Center for the Study of Community Colleges (CSCC) national faculty survey can be used to pose a wide variety of specific questions related to faculty characteristics, practices, and attitudes. This chapter will demonstrate that survey results can be used to ask broader questions concerning the development of the community college professoriate in the quarter-century since 1975, when the original CSCC faculty survey was administered. In addition, survey results can be used to draw broad implications for both research and practice. Accordingly, this chapter will use survey results related to a wide array of faculty practices and attitudes in an attempt to answer a fairly broad research question on the development of the community college professoriate: Have community college faculty developed a unified and distinct professional identity?

Two avenues of inquiry can be used to respond to this question. First, it would be useful to consider the results of the CSCC study within the context of the studies of professionalization of the community college professoriate to gain some insight into progress, or lack thereof, on such professionalization. As will be made evident, the work of three researchers in particular—Garrison, Cohen, and Brawer—is particularly relevant for this study. Second, we can consider an aspect of professionalization not

The author would like to acknowledge the community college presidents who agreed to participate in this study, the local facilitators who worked tirelessly to distribute and retrieve the surveys, and, above all, to the community college faculty respondents who found time in their busy schedules to make this study possible.

emphasized to date within the literature—internal unity among the professoriate[1]—and examine the internal differentiation revealed by the CSCC survey.

In Garrison's view (1967), community college instructors do not form a profession unto themselves, for several reasons. They cannot control the identity or number of students they teach; do not have time to fulfill their duties well; do not have access to adequate professional development; and work in isolation from one another. For Cohen and Brawer (1972), community colleges will not reach their full potential until their faculty become "professional" and "mature" (p. 4). Key elements of professionalization and maturation are self-management, independence, self-evaluation according to the ability to cause learning, and the provision of discrete services to a distinct clientele. Their repeated studies (1972, 1977, 1984) demonstrate that the faculty have not yet acquired these characteristics of professionalism.

To consider Garrison's criteria first, community college instructors have not achieved direct control over the students they serve, although many report that they would like a greater degree of such control. For example, just over half (50.7 percent) the respondents studied report that their courses would be improved through stricter admissions prerequisites, vs. just 4.8 percent who report that *fewer* prerequisites would improve their courses. On Garrison's criterion regarding insufficient time to fulfill their professional responsibilities, this study shows little progress. As reported above, nearly half (and a majority of full-timers) report that they feel "considerable stress" from their jobs. Other studies amply demonstrate that community college instructors suffer from a severe shortage of time (Seidman, 1985, Grubb, 1999). To consider Garrison's criterion regarding access to adequate professional development, just over half (50.6 percent) the respondents in this study have access to a formal orientation program. However, as other researchers note, these programs tend to be episodic at best and ineffectual at worst. Further, they are rarely oriented toward improving teaching, as Murray reports in Chapter Nine. Finally, to consider Garrison's contention that the faculty work in isolation, the CSCC study finds that faculty spend relatively little time with one another on activities related to teaching, and desire to spend even less. Only one-fifth of all faculty and 15 percent of part-timers report having taught jointly with a colleague outside of the respondent's department. Further, respondents report little informal interaction with colleagues outside the classroom, and few report desiring more such time with colleagues. In conclusion, then, community college faculty have not yet developed a distinct profession according to Garrison's criteria.

Cohen and Brawer's (1977) criteria for the formation of a profession are more abstract and less easily tested. However, results from the current study suggest that only mixed progress on these measures has been made since the mid-1970s. The debatable (Grubb, 1999) effect of unions aside, it is difficult to argue that faculty have acquired a greater ability to manage themselves than they had in 1975. Indeed, one could argue that faculty have fewer self-management abilities, given challenges to prerequisites and the increasing prevalence of part-timers, who typically have little or no authority in curricular and departmental issues.

Are the faculty independent? Again, it is difficult to provide a quantitative response to an abstract question of this type. It should be noted, as above, that the faculty do not have much control over the selection of their students, a majority express a preference for stricter prerequisites, and a majority report feeling considerable stress in their jobs. In another indication of dissatisfaction with the way they spend their time, over six times as many respondents (40.4 percent) report that they desire less time in administrative work than reported desiring more time in these activities (6.7 percent). More positively, the vast majority of respondents (81.9 percent) rate their ability to choose instructional materials as "excellent" or "good."

What of Cohen and Brawer's (1977) assertion that faculty should evaluate themselves according to their students' progress? Although the majority (60.3 percent) of instructors "somewhat" or "strongly" agree that their evaluations should be based in part on student evaluations, such evaluations are far from being based on the ability to cause student learning. However, survey findings do show that faculty are committed to effective instructional practice, as evidenced by their frequent syllabi revisions, provision of extracurricular activities, and use of a variety of instructional methods. More broadly, the use of classroom assessment techniques (Cross and Angelo, 1992) suggests that at least some faculty are willing to investigate the effectiveness of their instructional practice. The rising popularity of such practices offers hope that after decades of exhortation and rhetoric urging that they do so, the faculty are indeed developing a profession oriented toward effective teaching. In conclusion, on this measure of professionalism, as on the previous measures, results are mixed.

Cohen and Brawer (1977) offer one final hallmark of the formation of a distinct profession: the provision of discrete services to a distinct clientele. It is readily apparent that the distinctiveness of the clientele served by community college faculty exists in nominal form only. The population served by community college faculty can all be described as community college students, but this common label might be all that these students, the most diverse in higher education, have in common. However, it is less remarked that, apart from the title of community college instructor, little unites the disparate body of the community college professoriate.

The issue of internal differentiation brings us to a second means of considering the formation of community college instruction as a profession: the unity of the professoriate. Results from the CSCC study reflect an interesting and somewhat complex pattern of change and continuity in the community college professoriate. It is clear that community college faculty are both increasingly diverse and increasingly fragmented from one another.

While diversity in itself is certainly not an impediment to the formation of a cohesive group with a common sense of identity, the many significant differentiations in professional attitudes and practices noted above do present a challenge to the formation of a unified community college professoriate.

Other studies, including most of those in this volume, demonstrate that it is very difficult, if not impossible, to consider community college faculty as a monolithic group. Rather, the various subgroups that constitute the professoriate must be considered in their particularity. It is clear that the professoriate has grown increasingly fragmented since 1975, rather than developing as a distinct professional group. The further development of the professoriate's professional identity, as well as instructors' willingness to accept it as their own, is impeded by several forces: the rising prevalence of part-time instructors, the increased importance of the doctorate, the ever-expanding mission of the community colleges as extraeducational social agencies, and the corresponding pressure brought to bear on community college faculty to be involved in activities related to matters outside the domain of instruction.

Implications for Future Research

The current study did not investigate faculty professionalization within particular disciplines. Significant variations in the development of the professoriate might exist between departments. For example, are nursing faculty more or less professionalized than their counterparts in English? What are the consequences of such differentiation, if they indeed can be discerned? Consideration of these consequences leads naturally to a discussion of the practical implications of both the current study and future research avenues.

Implications for Practice

Is the professionalization of the community college professoriate inherently desirable? What are the real-world pedagogical consequences of this professionalization? Because of the complexity of both community college faculty and their professional mission, this is not an easy question to answer. However, contemplation of the first and still fundamental mission of the community colleges—teaching—suggests that professionalization, if oriented toward the centralization and improvement of instruction, is of value. Some students of the community colleges (see especially O'Banion, 1994) argue that community colleges must reemphasize their fundamental mission of teaching above all else. At the same time, Grubb (1999) finds that some community college instructors are evaluated in part on their research abilities while part-timers have assumed a much greater role within the professoriate. Taken together, these points suggest strongly that the enhancement of the community college professoriate as a profession that prioritizes teaching would be, in fact, of great benefit to community colleges' most important clients, their students, and that such enhancements are necessary now more than ever. Following are a few suggestions on means of effecting such enhancements.

Practical recommendations must be based on a firm understanding of the diversity of the faculty. Accordingly, it would behoove those concerned with the needs of these instructors to take their significant internal differentiations into account. (See Chapter Ten for a discussion of the creation of true community within community colleges.)

This study suggests that recommendations oriented toward part-timers could prove useful in ameliorating the working conditions not only of members of this group but of the professoriate as a whole. Many community college faculty, especially those employed part-time, work under conditions of isolation from one another, as demonstrated not only by this study, but also by Seidman (1985) and Grubb (1999). Grubb notes that this isolation is particularly acute for part-timers, as do Cohen and Brawer (1977) in their finding that part-timers are less likely to belong to professional organizations. The CSCC study finds that more and more instruction is delivered by instructors who spend less and less time on their campuses, probably because of the increasing prevalence of part-timers.

How can faculty isolation be countered? One way is through the provision of professional development programs with the twin goals of increasing interaction and promoting instructional effectiveness. Recommendations on these programs can be addressed to the distinct stakeholders who might be capable of effecting changes on campuses: administrators, faculty with administrative responsibilities (e.g., departmental chairs), and instructional faculty.

Administrators would do well to create professional development programs meant to bring faculty together in interaction with one another. These programs, particularly if they are oriented toward improving instructional abilities, would benefit not just the faculty but their students. Such programs would be considerably more effective than the episodic, unfocused offerings currently available (Grubb, 1999; see also Chapter Nine). As an additional benefit, professional development programs dedicated to instruction could counter the academic drift toward research and away from teaching (Quéval, 1990) that increasingly afflicts community colleges (Grubb, 1999), and would help to keep community colleges focused more closely on their original and enduring mission of teaching. As Zappia (1995) finds, community college faculty enjoy the instructional aspect of their jobs. What better way to promote satisfaction than by creating professional development programs to enhance an aspect of the profession that is already enjoyable?

It is all very well to suggest new development programs to administrators, but such unfunded mandates are unlikely to come to fruition. However, several zero-cost recommendations can be made to other stakeholders. Departmental chairs could take the simple step of inviting part-timers to departmental meetings, even if departmental policies and politics prohibit part-timers from voting. Failing this, department chairs could organize informal gatherings for faculty. If these sessions were held during those hours after the close of the usual workday yet before the beginning of evening classes, they might be effective in bringing together predominantly full-time day instructors with predominantly part-time evening instructors.

Finally, faculty development need not be formalized. Faculty themselves can assume responsibility for the well-being of their colleagues and the collegiality of their community. Faculty isolation and the fumbling, trial-and-error method by which many community college instructors learn to teach (Grubb, 1999) can be countered simply and effectively through one-on-one discussions between veterans and newcomers.

In conclusion, meeting the particular needs of all instructors via professional development would require not merely new programs but a new attitude toward part-timers on the part of administrators and faculty, and perhaps a new attitude from part-timers toward their institutions and colleagues. For these programs to be effective, part-timers, who are sometimes discouraged from participation in campus life (Gappa and Leslie, 1993), must be given adequate access to the support services accorded full-timers, and must be encouraged to engage in campus life more deeply than they report they do at present. In short, with part-timers now forming a majority of the community college professoriate (Cohen and Brawer, 1996; Palmer and Zimbler, 2000), it is no longer appropriate that institutions be structured as though full-time employment were the norm.

The recommendations offered above would decrease isolation and move the faculty closer to becoming, in Garrison's words, "a new breed of instructor in higher education," (Garrison, 1967, p. 15). Faculty isolation has hindered the professionalization of the community college professoriate; professional development programs that bring faculty into closer working relationships with one another could only contribute to the enhancement of the professoriate as a whole. If such programs were focused on teaching, the historically central role of teaching within the multiple missions of the community colleges could be affirmed.

Note

1. It should be noted, however, that internal unity was implicit in Cohen and Brawer's (1977) criterion of the provision of distinct services to a discrete population.

References

Cohen, A. M., and Brawer, F. B. *Confronting Identity: The Community College Instructor.* Englewood Cliffs, N.J.: Prentice Hall, 1972.

Cohen, A. M., and Brawer, F. B. *The Two-Year College Instructor Today.* New York: Holt, Rinehart and Winston, 1977.

Cohen, A. M., and Brawer, F. B. *The Collegiate Function of Community Colleges: Fostering Higher Learning Through Curriculum and Student Transfer.* San Francisco: Jossey-Bass, 1984.

Cohen, A. M., and Brawer, F. B. The *American Community College* (3rd ed.). San Francisco: Jossey-Bass, 1996.

Cross, K. P., and Angelo, T. A. *Classroom Assessment Techniques: A Handbook for Faculty.* Ann Arbor, Mich.: National Center for Research on the Improvement of Postsecondary Teaching and Learning, 1992.

Garrison, R. H. *Junior College Faculty: Issues and Problems; A Preliminary National Appraisal.* Washington, D.C.: American Association of Community and Junior Colleges, 1967.

Grubb, N. W. *Honored but Invisible: An Inside Look at Teaching in Community Colleges.* New York: Routledge, 1999.

O'Banion, T. (ed.). *Teaching and Learning in the Community College.* Washington, D.C.: American Association of Community Colleges, 1994.

Palmer, J. C., and Zimbler, L. J. *Instructional Faculty and Staff in Public 2-year Colleges.* Washington, D.C.: U.S. Department of Education, Office of Educational Research and Improvement, 2000.

Quéval, F. A. "The Evolution Toward Research Orientation and Capability in Comprehensive Universities. A Case Study: The California State University System." Unpublished doctoral dissertation, University of California-Los Angeles, 1990.

Seidman, E. *In the Words of the Faculty: Perspectives on Improving Teaching and Educational Quality in Community Colleges.* San Francisco: Jossey-Bass, 1985.

Zappia, C. A. "History in the 1990s: The Status of the Profession in the Community Colleges." Paper presented at the National Conference of the Community College Humanities Association, Washington, D.C., November 9–11, 1995. (ED 388 344).

CHARLES L. OUTCALT earned his Ph.D. from the Graduate School of Education and Information Studies at the University of California-Los Angeles in 2002. His dissertation offers a profile of community college faculty.

12

This annotated bibliography presents additional information related to community college faculty, including attitudes and perceptions, professional development, faculty evaluation, and recruitment.

Sources and Information: Community College Faculty

Michael Fleming

The sources presented in this chapter are recent documents from the ERIC database and issues related to community college faculty.[1] The recent literature tends to focus on four areas: faculty attitudes and perceptions, professional development, faculty evaluation, and faculty recruitment. But first, this chapter will note a few general sources that look at the overall demographics and profiles of community college faculty.

General Sources

Cohen, A. M., and Outcalt, C. L. "A Profile of the Community College Professoriate." A report submitted to the small research grants program of the Spencer Foundation. Los Angeles: Center for the Study of Community Colleges, 2001. (ED454930)

This study focuses on the nature and formation of a professional identity for the community college professoriate. Survey data show that faculty differ significantly on a wide variety of measures according to their personal and professional characteristics, including their instructional practices, levels of professional involvement, and use of professional reference groups. Some groups, most notably full-timers and doctorate seekers, demonstrate higher degrees of commitment to teaching, to their profession, and to their institutions. However, these same groups also report closer ties with four-year colleges and universities, a finding that contradicts the notion that community college instruction has developed as a professional practice *sui generis*. The authors conclude that the community college professoriate has become increasingly differentiated at the same time as the community college mission has grown ever more complex; however, it is not clear that the institutional mission and instructor practice have developed with close regard for each other.

Huber, M. T. Community College Faculty Attitudes and Trends, 1997 (R309A60001; NCPI-4–03). Stanford, Calif.: National Center for Postsecondary Improvement, 1998. (ED428796)

Huber highlights the status and working conditions of faculty in American community colleges and compares their responses to survey questions with those of faculty at research universities, graduate colleges and universities, and baccalaureate colleges. The report is organized around defining themes of academic life. The study provides a profile of the 5,151 respondents, including their demographic characteristics, education, current employment situation, and past careers. Results focus on faculty emphasis on teaching and learning, faculty views of students, satisfaction in teaching, faculty rewards in working at a teaching institution, evaluation of faculty roles, and the goals of community college education. The status of part-time faculty, faculty working conditions, faculty scholarship, governance, educational access and standards, and the role of higher education in society are also discussed.

Palmer, J. C., and Zimbler, L. J. *Instructional Faculty and Staff in Public 2-Year Colleges.* Washington, D.C.: U.S. Department of Education, Office of Educational Research and Improvement, 2000. (ED442518)

Data drawn from the 1993 National Study of Postsecondary Faculty is used to compare the backgrounds, teaching methods, and careers of instructional faculty and staff at public two-year colleges. Differences by age (under thirty-five vs. fifty-five to sixty-four), years of experience (under ten years vs. twenty or more years), and primary teaching field are examined. Results indicate gradual changes in the nature of the community college instructional enterprise, with no watershed change apparent in teaching methods as the new generation of teachers replaces those who began in the 1960s and early 1970s.

Snyder, T. D., and Hoffman, C. M. *Digest of Education Statistics, 2000.* Washington, D.C.: National Center for Education Statistics, 2001. (ED455275)

This publication provides a compilation of statistical information covering the broad field of U.S. education from kindergarten through graduate school. Data are drawn from both government and private sources. The information provided includes the number of schools and colleges, teachers, enrollments, graduates, educational finances, federal funds for education, employment and income of graduates, libraries, and international education. Supplemental information on population trends, attitudes toward education, education characteristics of the labor force, government finances, and economic trends are also provided. The publication includes data on faculty demographics, salaries, perceptions, and other information. The report is available online at [http://nces.ed.gov/pubs2001/digest/].

Faculty Attitudes and Perceptions

Faculty attitudes, perceptions, and satisfaction regarding community colleges, teaching, and community college students continue to interest researchers. Numerous studies, including those in the preceding chapters of this volume, have recently been conducted on faculty satisfaction, sources of stress, involvement in governance, instructional innovation, and attitudes about evaluation.

Brewer, D. J. "How Do Community College Faculty View Institutional Mission? An Analysis of National Survey Data." Community College Research Center report. New York: Columbia University, 1999. (ED440695)
    Brewer presents the results of a national survey of 1,725 community college faculty at 92 institutions. The respondents are asked about their views of institutional missions and future directions of their institutions. Some argue that multiple offerings improve educational opportunities for students, while others suggest that multiple missions and activities lead to a lack of clear purpose and less effective institutions. Many faculty are not supportive of community colleges continuing to expand noncredit activities along with increased basic and remedial course offerings. The marginalization of these activities, with respect to traditional academic and vocational missions, may lead to increasing disputes over appropriate resource allocation. Survey results lend support to the idea that faculty operate as independent islands with relatively little intercommunication. The report concludes by saying that given changing student demographics, the demand for noncredit activities will likely grow and colleges should find ways to integrate faculty into these efforts.

Fugate, A. L., and Amey, M. "Career Stages of Community College Faculty: A Qualitative Analysis of Their Career Paths, Roles, and Development." Community College Review, 2000, 28(1), 1–22. (EJ611809)
    Qualitative interviews with twenty-two community college faculty members yield information about their perceptions of their career paths, early-stage career roles, and the role played by faculty development. Results suggest that the majority of faculty choose the community college because of its emphasis on teaching. Faculty also report that their roles and career goals change over time, generally from a focus on research to instruction of students, student development, and achievement. Based on the findings, the authors propose recommendations to enhance faculty recruitment, retention, and development.

Townsend, B., and LaPaglia, N. "Are We Marginalized Within Academe? Perceptions of Two-Year College Faculty." *Community College Review,* 2000, 28(1),41–48. (EJ611811)

A sample of 311 faculty at seven community colleges answer survey questions that elicit faculty ratings of statements about four-year-institution faculty attitudes toward two-year-college faculty and about their own perceptions of their status within academe.

Respondents with prior full-time faculty experience at four-year institutions are more likely to agree than those without such experience that four-year faculty consider two-year faculty to be on the margins of higher education. Members of neither group consider themselves to be in a marginal position. The authors discuss the implications of the data and make recommendations for future research.

Valadez, J. R., and Anthony, J. S. "Job Satisfaction and Commitment of Two-Year College Part-Time Faculty." *Community College Journal of Research and Practice,* 2001 25(2), 97–108. (EJ623666)

The authors analyze survey data from 6,811 two-year-college part-time faculty about their job satisfaction and commitment, collected from the 1992–1993 National Study of Postsecondary Faculty. Findings indicate that part-time community college faculty are satisfied with their instructional roles but are concerned with issues regarding salary, benefits, and long-term job security. The study also includes perceptions and demographic information about age, ethnicity, and educational level of part-time faculty.

Professional Development

Faculty members are constantly questioned and evaluated on topics such as student achievement and the quality of instruction. One way community colleges are tackling the issues is through the use of professional development programs for faculty. Some of the programs community colleges are utilizing include training manuals, instruction seminars, and mentor programs for new faculty. The following sources identify and address a few of the typical and growing issues for professional development programs.

Carreiro, J., Guffey, J. S., and Rampp, L. C. "A Paradigm for the Training of Part-Time Teachers in Community Colleges." Unpublished doctoral dissertation, Arkansas State University, 1999. (ED436194)

The authors identify and survey seventy-seven community colleges from twenty-seven states that have staff development programs for part-time teachers. They analyze specific aspects and common components included in these programs and also provide information on overall student enrollment and the number of part-time faculty members at each community college. Conclusions from the study present a paradigm or suggested design that should be contained in any effective staff development program for training part-time adjunct teachers in community colleges.

Grubb, N. W. *Honored but Invisible: An Inside Look at Teaching in Community Colleges.* New York: Routledge, 1999. (ED435430)

This study of teaching in community colleges is based on classroom observation and interviews of 257 instructors and 60 administrators at thirty-two community colleges across the country. It emphasizes the collective nature of teaching, the influence of peer networks, and the culture and incentives that exist within the community colleges. The author makes recommendations for improving the teaching culture of community colleges, such as revised personnel practices, greater administrative commitment to teaching, and the development of in-service education and staff development.

Murray, J. P. "Faculty Development in a National Sample of Community Colleges." *Community College Review,* 1999, 27(3), 47–64. (EJ602056)

Murray defines the activities that distinguish successful faculty development programs and describes a survey completed in 1998 by faculty development officers at 130 randomly selected community colleges. The article profiles those responsible for faculty development, summarizes the extent to which each development activity is used, and articulates the need for concerted faculty development efforts at community colleges. Findings include suggestions and recommendations for instructional workshops, technical training of faculty, and research opportunities.

Faculty Evaluation

Another way in which community colleges are addressing the question of ensuring high-quality instruction is by utilizing new techniques to evaluate faculty. In the past, schools relied more on students and administrators, but now community colleges often incorporate faculty into the evaluating process based on the belief that doing so will lead to a more thorough, fair, and effective evaluation process and ultimately increase the quality of instruction and faculty responsibility for student learning.

Miller, R. I., Finley, C., and Vancko, C. S. *Evaluating, Improving, and Judging Faculty Performance in Two-Year Colleges.* Westport, Conn.: Bergin and Garvey, 2000. (ED439758)

This book provides a comprehensive picture of how community college faculty can be effectively evaluated in order to improve instruction at two-year institutions. The authors look at ways to prepare instructors for the next century and outline future needs that will significantly affect thoughts and plans concerning the improvement of community college faculty performance. Appendices provide valuable supplementary materials for community college faculty and administration.

Redmon, K. D. "ERIC Review. Faculty Evaluation in Community Colleges: A Response to Competing Values." *Community College Review,* 1999, 27(1), 57–71. (EJ590044)

The author reviews the literature related to evaluation of community college faculty within the context of "competing values" between administrators and faculty. Examples of competing values include differing opinions on productivity, student needs, and achievement. Two evaluation approaches emerge from the literature: (1) a "procedural approach," which combines self-evaluations with ongoing appraisals made by peers, administrators, and students to accumulate a body of evidence that is used for both formative and summative appraisals, and (2) a "developmental approach," where faculty create teaching portfolios, dossiers, and self-evaluations that describe teaching strengths and accomplishments while participating in faculty development programs. The author suggests that a combined model may be the best solution for appraising faculty performance.

Faculty Recruitment

Research has shown that the faculty at most community colleges are "graying" and nearing retirement (approximately three-fourths of full-time community college faculty will retire within the next twenty years). These institutions are addressing this issue by seeking new strategies to attract and recruit new faculty by using outside consultants, existing faculty, and information surveys. Recruiting diverse faculty as well as instructors with professional expertise and experience is still a concern of most community colleges.

Brewster, D. "The Use of Part-Time Faculty in the Community College." *Inquiry*, 2000, 5(1), 66–76. (EJ610224)

The author examines the problem of increasing reliance on part-time faculty and discusses various issues relating to the employment of part-time faculty. Brewster prioritizes six practices in handling and preparing part-time faculty: recruitment, selection, orientation, staff development, evaluation, and integration. The author maintains that effective communication is the required common element in all six processes and suggests building a sense of belonging in part-time faculty as a way to improve job performance and satisfaction.

Manzo, K. K. "Faculty Lounge: Community College Faculty." *Black Issues in Higher Education*, 2000, 17(13), 54–57. (EJ614991)

Manzo suggests that many scholars of color are drawn to community colleges because of the emphasis on teaching and the more diverse student population present on most campuses. The author discusses concerns related to locating, recruiting, and keeping faculty of color, as well as the difficulty of community college faculty in finding time for research. A list of the top fifty community colleges with the highest number and percentage of African-American faculty for the fall of 1997 is provided.

Murray, J. P. "Interviewing to Hire Competent Community College Faculty." *Community College Review*, 1999, 27(1), 41–56. (EJ90043)

This article focuses on improving the interview process as a critical step in hiring new faculty who will prove to be effective in the community college environment. Murray defines the necessary considerations for preplanning, establishing an interview protocol, and developing interview questions based upon a review of the literature and suggests garnering and utilizing input from faculty on relevant questions to be asked during interviews.

Rifkin, T. "Public Community College Faculty. New Expeditions: Charting the Second Century of Community Colleges." Issues paper no. 4. AACC report. Washington D.C.: American Association of Community Colleges, 2000. (ED439739)

This paper addresses the graying of faculty, faculty recruitment and retention, roles and responsibilities, evaluation, professionalism, and issues related to part-time faculty. According to the author, the student body of today's community colleges is tremendously diverse, making the recruitment and retention of new faculty even more complicated. The secondary school, the traditional community college faculty source of teachers, is not as dependable as in the past. As approximately three-fourths of full-time community college faculty will retire within the next twenty years, community colleges will have to recruit from a pool of applicants who will best serve the ever-increasing diverse population.

Note

1. Most ERIC documents (publications with ED number) can be viewed on microfiche at over nine hundred libraries worldwide. In addition, most may be ordered on microfiche or on paper from the ERIC Document Reproduction Service (EDRS) by calling (800) 443-ERIC. Journal articles are not available from EDRS, but they can be acquired through regular library channels or purchased from one of the following article reproduction services: Carl Uncover: [http://www.carl.org/uncover], uncover@carl.org, (800) 787-7979; UMI: orders@infostore.com, (800) 248-0360; or IDI: tga@isinet.com, (800) 523-1850.

MICHAEL FLEMING is a doctoral student in the Graduate School of Education and Information Studies at the University of California–Los Angeles.

INDEX

Back Issue/Subscription Order Form

Copy or detach and send to:

Jossey-Bass, A Wiley Company, 989 Market Street, San Francisco CA 94103-1741

Call or fax toll-free: Phone 888-378-2537 6AM-5PM PST; Fax 888-481-2665

Back issues: Please send me the following issues at $28 each.

(Important: please include series initials and issue number, such as CC114)

1. CC _____

_____

_____

$ _____Total for single issues

$ _____SHIPPING CHARGES: SURFACE

	Domestic	Canadian
First Item	$5.00	$6.50
Each Add'l Item	$3.00	$3.00

For next-day and second-day delivery rates, call the number listed above.

Subscriptions: Please ❑ start ❑ renew my subscription to *New Directions for Community Colleges* for the year 2____ at the following rate:

U.S.	❑ Individual $66	❑ Institutional $135
Canada	❑ Individual $66	❑ Institutional $175
All Others	❑ Individual $90	❑ Institutional $209

$ _____Total single issues and subscriptions (Add appropriate sales tax for your state for single issue orders. No sales tax for U.S. subscriptions. Canadian residents, add GST for subscriptions and single issues.)

Federal Tax ID 135593032   GST 89102 8052

❑ Payment enclosed (U.S. check or money order only)

❑ VISA, MC, AmEx, Discover Card # _____ Exp. date_____

Signature _____ Day phone _____

❑ Bill me (U.S. institutional orders only. Purchase order required)

Purchase order #_____

Name _____

Address _____

_____

Phone_____ E-mail _____

For more information about Jossey-Bass, visit our Web site at: www.josseybass.com

PROMOTION CODE = ND3

CC112   Beyond Access: Methods and Models for Increasing Retention and
         Learning Among Minority Students
         Steven R.. Aragon
         Presents practical models, alternative approaches, and new strategies for
         creating effective cross-cultural courses that foster higher retention and
         learning success for minority students. Argues that educational programs
         must now develop a broader curriculum that includes multicultural and
         multi-linguistic information.
         ISBN: 0-7879-5429-2

CC111   How Community Colleges Can Create Productive Collaborations with
         Local Schools
         James C. Palmer
         Details ways that community colleges and high schools can work together to
         help students navigate the difficult passage from secondary to higher
         education. Provides detailed case studies of actual collaborations between
         specific community colleges and high school districts, discusses legal
         problems that can arise when high school students enroll in community
         colleges, and more.
         ISBN: 0-7879-5428-4

CC110   Building Successful Relationships Between Community Colleges and the
         Media
         Clifton Truman Daniel, Hanel Henriksen Hastings
         Explores current relationships between two-year colleges and the media
         across the country, reviewing the history of community colleges'
         relationships with members of the press, examining the media's relationships
         with community college practitioners, and offering practical strategies for
         advancing an institution's visibility.
         ISBN: 0-7879-5427-6

CC109   Dimensions of Managing Academic Affairs in the Community College
         Douglas Robillard, Jr.
         Offers advice on fulfilling the CAO's academic duties, and explores the
         CAO's faculty and administrative roles, discussing how to balance the
         sometimes conflicting roles of faculty mentor, advocate, and disciplinarian
         and the importance of establishing a synergistic working relationship with
         the president.
         ISBN: 0-7879-5369-5

CC108   Trends in Community College Curriculum
         Gwyer Schuyler
         Presents a detailed picture of the national community college curriculum,
         using survey data collected in 1998 by the Center for the Study of
         Community Colleges. Chapters analyze approaches to general education,
         vocational course offerings, the liberal arts, multicultural education, ESL,
         honors programs, and distance learning.
         ISBN: 0-7879-4849-7

CC107   Gateways to Democracy: Six Urban Community College Systems
         Raymond C. Bowen, Gilbert H. Muller
         Features case studies of six prototypical urban community college systems,
         exploring how they meet the educational and training needs of an
         increasingly diverse ethnic and racial community.
         ISBN: 0-7879-4848-9

CC106 **Understanding the Impact of Reverse Transfer Students on Community Colleges**
Barbara K. Townsend
Examines institutions' strategies for recruiting, retaining, and serving reverse transfer students and reveals how the presence of reverse transfer students affects policy-making.
ISBN: 0-7879-4847-0

CC105 **Preparing Department Chairs for Their Leadership Roles**
Rosemary Gillett-Karam
Presents the qualities that experienced department chairs cite as being crucial to success and makes a persuasive argument for the need to develop formal training programs for people newly appointed to these positions.
ISBN: 0-7879-4846-2

CC104 **Determining the Economic Benefits of Attending Community College**
Jorge R. Sanchez, Frankie Santos Laanan
Discusses various state initiatives that look at student outcomes and institutional accountability efforts and analyzes the trend to connect accountability and outcome measures with funding.
ISBN: 0-7879-4237-5

CC103 **Creating and Benefiting from Institutional Collaboration: Models for Success**
Dennis McGrath
Examines the many ways collaboration both benefits and alters the participating organizations, offering practical examples and lessons learned that can be used by a variety of institutions in their efforts to foster collaborative relationships.
ISBN: 0-7879-4236-7

CC102 **Organizational Change in the Community College: A Ripple or a Sea Change?**
John Stewart Levin
Presents real-life examples of community colleges' experiences with organizational change—both successful and unsuccessful—and examines organizational change through a variety of theoretical frameworks, including feminism and postmodernism.
ISBN: 0-7879-4235-9

CC101 **Integrating Technology on Campus: Human Sensibilities and Technical Possibilities**
Kamala Anandam
Addresses the topics of organizational structures, comprehensive economic planning, innovative policies and procedures, faculty development, and above all, collaborative approaches to achieving significant and enduring results from technological applications.
ISBN: 0-7879-4234-0

CC100 **Implementing Effective Policies for Remedial and Developmental Education**
Jan M. Ignash
Addresses specific policy questions involved in the debate over remedial and developmental education and uses national and state data, as well as information from case studies of individual institutions, to provide insights into effective approaches to remedial and developmental education.
ISBN: 0-7879-9843-5

CC99 **Building a Working Policy for Distance Education**
Connie L. Dillon, Rosa Cintron
Presents some of the policy issues confronting higher education in the age of
distance learning, and discusses the implications of these issues for the
community college.
ISBN: 0-7879-9842-7

CC98 **Presidents and Trustees in Partnership: New Roles and Leadership
Challenges**
Iris M. Weisman, George B. Vaughan
Explores the professional needs, challenges, and roles of community college
governing board members and their presidents—and how these factors
influence the board-president team.
ISBN: 0-7879-9818-4

CC97 **School-to-Work Systems: The Role of Community Colleges in Preparing
Students and Facilitating Transitions**
Edgar I. Farmer, Cassy B. Key
Demonstrates how community colleges are engaged in strengthening
existing partnerships with schools, employers, and labor- and community-
based organizations as they develop new programs to address the three
major components of school-to-work systems.
ISBN: 0-7879-9817-6

CC96 **Transfer and Articulation: Improving Policies to Meet New Needs**
Tronie Rifkin
Presents recommendations for current and future transfer and articulation
policies in an attempt to expand the discourse and thereby enhance the
ability of community colleges to serve their own educational goals as well as
the educational goals of this nation.
ISBN: 0-7879-9893-1

CC95 **Graduate and Continuing Education for Community College Leaders:
What It Means Today**
James C. Palmer, Stephen G. Katsinas
Provides critical perspectives on the current status of community college
education as an academic specialty.
ISBN: 0-7879-9892-3

CC89 **Gender and Power in the Community College**
Barbara K. Townsend
Examines the gender socialization that results in stereotypes that usually
operate to women's disadvantage socially, politically, and economically and
explores ways the community college experience can be structured to
overcome this disadvantage.
ISBN: 0-7879-9913-X

CC77 **Critical Thinking: Educational Imperative**
Cynthia A. Barnes
Considers ways in which high-level thinking skills can be integrated with
content and taught across institutional disciplines and means by which
instructors and administrators can become involved in these efforts.
ISBN: 1-55542-749-9